Vulnerable Witness

Vulnerable Witness

The Politics of Grief in the Field

Edited by Kathryn Gillespie and
Patricia J. Lopez

UNIVERSITY OF CALIFORNIA PRESS

University of California Press, one of the most distin-
guished university presses in the United States, enriches
lives around the world by advancing scholarship in the
humanities, social sciences, and natural sciences. Its
activities are supported by the UC Press Foundation and
by philanthropic contributions from individuals and
institutions. For more information, visit www.ucpress.edu.

University of California Press
Oakland, California

Library of Congress Cataloging-in-Publication Data

Names: Gillespie, Kathryn (Kathryn A.), author. |
    Lopez, Patricia J., author.
Title: Vulnerable witness : the politics of grief in the field
    / Kathryn Gillespie and Patricia J. Lopez.
Description: Oakland, California : University of
    California Press, [2019] | Includes bibliographical
    references and index. |
Identifiers: LCCN 2018057019 (print) | LCCN 2019001881
    (ebook) | ISBN 9780520970038 (e-book) |
    ISBN 9780520297845 (cloth : alk. paper) |
    ISBN 9780520297852 (pbk : alk. paper)
Subjects: LCSH: Grief—Political aspects. | Research—
    Political aspects. | Research—Psychological aspects.
Classification: LCC BF575.G7 (ebook) | LCC BF575.G7 G545
    2019 (print) | DDC 155.9/37—dc23
LC record available at https://lccn.loc.gov/2018057019

29 27 26 25 24 23 22 21 20 19
10 9 8 7 6 5 4 3 2 1

CONTENTS

ACKNOWLEDGMENTS

This book would not have been possible without the input of too many interlocutors, colleagues, friends, and invisible others with whom we have shared this project to name them all individually. We extend our utmost gratitude to the courageous panelists and audience members who participated in the panels "Grieving Witnesses: The Politics of Grief in the Field I & II" at the 2015 annual meeting of the American Association of Geographers. We especially thank Kate Coddington, Dana Cuomo, Kalli F. Doubleday, Maureen Hays-Mitchell, Lakhbir K. Jassal, Jacquelyn Micieli-Voutsinas, Helen Olsen, Elizabeth A. Olson, Matthew Rosenblum, Audra L. Vilaly, Jessie Hanna Clark, Michelle D. Daigle, Christine Eriksen, Lauri Heffron, Catherine L. Nolan, and William Payne, who shared their stories and insights, inviting others to do the same. And a special thanks to the authors who shared with us their stories in the form of chapters for this book and to those who have shared conversations about grief in their research and fieldwork. We are also grateful to Pamela Moss and Kye Askins for their constructive and supportive suggestions for strengthening this work; to Naomi Schneider at University of California Press for shepherding the book through to publication; to Benjy Malings at University of California Press for keeping us on track; and to Avril Maddrell and Maureen Hays-Mitchell for encouraging us to publish a collection on this subject in the first place. Finally, a heartfelt thanks for the loving support of our partners. Tish would like to thank Jason MacLeod, Émile, and Sir Marx-a-Lot for their unending patience and companionship through this collection's many iterations. Katie would like to thank Eric Haberman, Saoirse, Lucy, and Amelia, and Abigail and Eden for offering so much love, support, and a deep sense of family every day.

Introduction

PATRICIA J. LOPEZ AND
KATHRYN GILLESPIE

The inspiration for this book is rooted in informal conversations we have engaged in over the years with other scholars and activists about the emotional toll of grief experienced by those who engage in social justice–oriented research and advocacy. One of the catalysts for these conversations was a searing experience of grief we shared when we attended a farmed animal auction yard together in June 2012, beginning what we have come to call a "buddy system" approach to research.[1] Although this was not the first (or the last) time we both experienced grief in our research, our shared grieving at the auction and the way our grief ran counter to the dominant affective nature of the auction yard itself made us pause more than once to reflect on the role of grief in fieldwork.

As we have written about elsewhere, auction yards are routine spaces of exchange for animal agriculture and are not typically framed as spaces of human grief.[2] At the auction yard, we witnessed cows raised for dairy collapse in the auction ring and holding pens; cows and their calves sold separately, bellowing to each other across the pens; day-old calves with their umbilical cords still dangling from their bellies who were being sold for veal production and were attempting to nuzzle the auctioneer; and cows being beaten and shocked with electric prods. These routine features of animal agriculture (dairy and meat production) are so thoroughly normalized that they are not viewed as violence against the animal.[3] Farmed animals' lives and deaths are routinely rendered ungrievable through this normalization of violence against them.[4] Our own overwhelming grief in confronting the suffering experienced by cows at the auction yard caused us to reflect together on questions of grievability, ethics, and our role as researchers and academics. Questions posed by Judith Butler about the political nature of grief—of grieving the ungrievable—were at the forefront of our conversations: How did grieving the "spent" cow raised for dairy, collapsed from exhaustion in the auction pen, make political her life, commodification, and death?[5] What did it mean for us to be there, witnessing her, grieving for her, and doing nothing to change the trajectory of her fate? How could we process and make manifest this grief when grieving the lives and deaths of farmed animals is, as James Stanescu explains, "socially unintelligible"?[6]

As we thought about these questions, we were also talking with others about their experiences of grief in the field and found that many of them were struggling with similar questions. It was these experiences that led us to organize a set of sessions at the 2015 annual meeting of the American Association of Geographers in Chicago, Illinois. There was such an overwhelming response to the call for panelists that the sessions spanned the better part of a day, and, with many others who came to present and listen, we engaged in an intimate, dynamic, and moving conversation on themes of grief, trauma, emotion, and witnessing in fieldwork. At the end of the sessions, we were asked by a number of people to "do something more" with the conversations that were sparked in the sessions; there was an urgent sense among participants and attendees that these ideas and experiences should be shared beyond the conversations in that room and offered up as a resource for other researchers and advocates. To be sure, feminist scholars and ethnographers have published well-theorized academic works on some of these themes; indeed, this volume follows on a genealogy of intimate looks at trauma, loss, and grief in the field, such as Renato Rosaldo's *Culture and Truth*, Carmen Diana Deere and Diane Wolf's edited collection *Feminist Dilemmas in Fieldwork*, and Ruth Behar's *The Vulnerable Observer.*[7] What stood out about these sessions was the raw emotion, solidarity, and ethic of care involved as individuals shared their experiences in a way that did not require them to maintain a facade of rational or distant academic-researcher. Rather, the emotions felt were acknowledged openly as a valid response to the violence witnessed in the field.

For many, this open sharing and acknowledgment prompted an enormous sense of relief just to know that others, even if they did not actively share those same field experiences, could identify with the toll of their own work on their mental and emotional well-being. Woven through these stories were the loneliness and feelings of madness that emerge when trying to push away these emotions or pretend they are not there in order to perform the perfectly disciplined, productive, neoliberal subject (the poised and professional teacher, the prolific writer, the prestigious grants recipient, the well-spoken presenter, the unfazed conservationist). The act of grieving in and after "the field" disrupts this flow of neoliberal productivity, forcing a slowing down or, at times, even a stoppage. A number of participants in these discussions expressed the difficulty they had experienced getting to the act of writing or even returning to their everyday lives because it meant facing the traumatic nature of their research and working through the grief that was there, just below the surface (which would bubble up, usually at the most inopportune times).

As we moved from these conference sessions into formulating the project in book form, we began with a list of more than forty scholars, practitioners, and activists—most of whom we have met, some of whom were recommended to us by others. As we sought contributors, the initial response was strong, and many replied enthusiastically that they would love to participate. Only a handful declined at the outset, usually out of concern for other pressing engagements. But as the weeks and months went by, the silence from some authors was resoundingly loud. One by one, we received e-mails from, or had conversations at conferences with, authors who admitted that the very act of attempting to write their grief had raised unresolved emotions and traumas. Some laughed nervously, noting that the act of trying to confront and understand their grief forced them to acknowledge their need for counseling. Others teared up or wept openly as they shared their struggles. The pain that the possibility of this dialogue opened up was raw and palpable. But it wasn't pain created by broaching the subject; it was pain that seeped from the deep wounds that were already there.

In the work of bringing together so many grieving authors, it has become clear to us that many people struggle to make the time to take care of themselves, of their own emotional needs. In nursing and social work, this is known as the "self-care deficit"— a take on care ethicists' concerns for the "care deficit," or the vacuum of care left when a primary caregiver enters the workforce. Through this lens, then, it is plain that many academics, activists, and practitioners have taken up the insistence on productivity over self-care.[8] There simply is not time for self-care *now*, given the pressing deadlines and temporal strictures of life in late liberal capitalism and, more pointedly, in the neoliberal academy.

Challenges related to self-care and mental and emotional well-being are not unique to the call for this volume; rather, they are situated within a growing conversation about the mental health crisis in academia. Indeed, a recent study summarized in *Times Higher Education* suggests that academics "face higher mental health risks" than those working in other professions.[9] And while none in the profession could confess to being surprised, perhaps bell hooks most clearly defines this mind-body-spirit split the academy expects of its faculty, noting that "the self [i]s presumably emptied out the moment the threshold [i]s crossed, leaving in place only an objective mind—free of experiences and biases."[10] To refuse this framing, to center not just emotion itself but the moments in which emotions have interrupted, swayed, pushed, and stopped our work as researchers, is to center a recognition of the very political nature of emotions in the field. With the exception of some recently published feminist scholarship, emotional responses to research and advocacy have largely been left to informal conversations. Our hope in publishing this collection is that the deep emotional resonances that reverberate across the somatic, intellectual, and affective self might be taken more seriously while also reminding researchers and practitioners that they are not alone.[11]

GUIDING QUESTIONS

In offering a space for these expressions of grief, we posed a series of interrelated questions, drawing together witnessing, responsibility, ethics, grief, and self-care. For us, the questions posed were not intended as outlines, nor were they imbued with expectations. They were invitations to ruminate, to think aloud, to feel publicly, to respond from and to the moments (and sometimes extended periods) of grief that emerge in the midst of "doing research"—either in the actual field or in private lives. We have chosen to leave these sets of questions as we posed them to the researchers in order not to theorize each framing in a top-down way, but rather to open up the frame for theory to emerge through the questions and through the very act of storytelling; importantly, "stories are material practices" and are the theory in themselves as living discourse.[12] In turn, we have asked our authors to loosen their grip on theory. This proved to be difficult in some cases. In the end, for some authors, a reliance on theorizing their grief to the elision of their own personal frames took over—we learned through this process the work that turgid theorizing can do within the affective realm; namely, it offers a way to depersonalize and distance the personal or to create a protective shell around one's emotional core. For other authors, distancing occurred through a reliance on ephemeral expressions of "our grief" as opposed to their own, framing their singular experiences within a broader community of academics, activists, and practitioners. Within an institution that is often hostile to expressions of emotion or vulnerability, it can feel safer and less dangerous to couch one's own, singular experience in expressions of the "we." For yet another author, her inability to write about the trauma itself led to a piece about how she attempts to engage in self-care. Together, the framing questions and the chapter responses have turned away from this disciplined reliance on theory for legibility and instead seek to offer further opening.

Researchers are often in the position of bearing witness to suffering or injustice—a position that frequently highlights their privilege and the uneven power relations between researcher and researched, witness and witnessed.[13] *What is the relationship between the witness and the witnessed? What are researchers' responsibilit to those whose lives they witness? What are the ethics and responsibilities involved in witnessing? How do researchers reconcile the differential acceptance of suffering for different bodies, especially where "acceptable suffering" has varied norms and normalizing functionality across a range of geographies?*

In critical research, researchers often feel that they have a responsibility to be involved in social, economic, and political change—perhaps even engaging as public intellectuals.[14] *What are researchers' responsibilities to intervene when they encounter intimate violence and suffering, and how might they try to shift more structural aspects of violence? In other words, how do researchers see themselves not just as academic scholars but as scholar-activists dedicated to changing the conditions they study? How do scholar-activists research in service to those they study? How do they collaborate with those groups they study to make change in the moment and in broader structural conditions?*

Humans, of course, are not the only species that engages in grief; nonhuman animals, too, grieve deeply from trauma they experience, and, as for humans, grieving for other species and ecosystems is often rendered socially unintelligible.[15] Grieving the ungrievable is intertwined with ethical questions about proximity and responsibility to human and nonhuman others. *What are the ethics of grieving and witnessing? Who has the right to grieve? And for how long (e.g., we are thinking about cross-generational trauma among elephant and other animal populations, among human populations after Hurricane Katrina, in instances of genocide, etc.)? How does one engage in grieving at a distance, whether that distance is temporal, cultural, physical, or across sites of perceived difference (race, gender, sexuality, species, etc.)?*

The weight of uncovering the depths of structural violence as researchers seek to understand the production of suffering sometimes provokes them to recognize their own embeddedness in these structures of violence and, especially, the fact that even as they try to live their lives as people and scholars in ever more ethical ways, they are also still deeply embedded in practices and processes that do harm.[16] In fact, they often benefit from certain forms of violence and structures of power, operating with various forms of inherited privilege (racial, class, species). *How does one reconcile this privilege and one's embeddedness in violent social relations so that it is possible to move forward but also acknowledge that there is always more to be done? How does one not become hardened by the constant barrage of images of atrocities or by witnessing firsthand the suffering of others? And conversely, how do researchers not become burned out by the work (i.e., by feeling it too much to sustain the work)? What are the tools they engage in (successfully or not) to protect themselves? What is the role of guilt, and how do researchers intentionally make their grief and the grief of others political? Finally—and this is important—how do researchers who study violent social relations have hope?*

WITNESSING, ENTANGLEMENTS, AND CO-OCCURRING EMOTIONS

For scholars who study death and dying, violence and killing, suffering and injustice, and marginalization and dispossession, grief and the act of grieving are often central, politically, to the research process, and yet, this emotional labor and its politics are rarely centered in our work. In this collection, the authors are all writing about their personal emotional responses that have emerged through their work and as witnesses while in the field or in practice. In this, these are not generalized accounts of personal experiences in academia or in contact zones related to academia, nor are they empirical accounts or analyses of the work they have engaged in. Rather, the authors reflect on their personal emotional reactions with the settings, scenes, people, nonhuman animals, environments, and material that they encounter. As emotional beings who care deeply about the subjects we study, we often grieve the injustices we encounter and the illegibility of this grief when the bodies and lives we grieve are deemed "ungrievable." Often, our processes and experiences of grief are sidelined or dismissed as personal emotional responses—not relevant to our research, or even antithetical to it. And yet, as Judith Butler and others continue to remind us in a broader landscape of the politics of emotion: grief is a political act with political implications.[17] When we acknowledge grief not merely as a solipsistic reflection on our own emotional state but as an act of recognition, the political nature of both the subject we are grieving and the grieving process itself can emerge.[18]

Grief is often regulated through processes of normalization through the "violence of derealization."[19] Complex emotions and their entanglements within and through research are often elided, erased, or ignored in the service of academic productivity, global conservation, and professional attitudes. Grief is often only legible when it is collective grief—the grief of a nation, a group, and ecologies that have experienced a pointed political economic violence that is knowable to a wider audience that acknowledges that violence *as* violence.[20] To experience grief alone, or for those who might be deemed "others," is seen as an aberration outside the scope of what might be deemed normal.[21]

So, too, grief often comes with silent temporal rules—both real and perceived. Although many of the authors studiously avoided discussions of the temporal throughout their narratives, there is an underlying neoliberal insistence to return to work, to not be pulled too far out of the strict timelines we often face.[22] Grief and mourning generate new temporalities that lose their linearity.[23] The past haunts an almost imperceptible present, even as it is girded by an impending future. Indeed, grief is often a response that finds no home in the workplace. To return to the work of working, grief must be sequestered. And yet, as Butler reminds us: "One cannot say, 'Oh, I'll go through this loss this way, and that will be the result, and I'll apply myself to that task, and I'll endeavor to achieve the resolution of grief that is before me.' I think one is hit by the waves, and that one starts out the day with an aim, a project, a plan, and finds oneself foiled. One finds oneself fallen."[24] This metaphor of grief as a series of waves, undulating at its own tempo, is not uncommon.[25] Grief is a common reaction to loss, to witnessing others' losses and the loss of biodiversity. It is affective and embodied—sometimes private and sometimes public, but always personal.[26]

Within late liberalism and its attendant neoliberal subjectification and domination, public grief of the personal kind is disallowed—and this refusal to allow grief is a mechanism of discipline and violence that prescribes who can grieve, how, and in what spaces.[27] Storytelling and narratives of experiences in the field call for foregrounding the power of emotion and the pervasiveness of grief in our research. In privileging the varied embodied emotional responses that take grief as their starting point, we open up the frame to the lived realities of many of our colleagues—not to normalize it but to *denormalize* abjection. In some small ways, this collection is a reminder that grief does not simply slip away, personalized and forgotten to all but those who have grieved. It is an invitation to acknowledge grief in its many forms. It is an attempt to recenter the very essence of what it means to live inside of affective bodies and experiences.

Grief is also geographic. The spaces, places, and scales in which grief occurs shape the manifestation, processing, and understanding of grief and mourning.[28] Grief transforms spaces into places as they become "endowed with *meaning and significance*" through grief—transformations that can be either personal or collective.[29] Grief travels geographically, creating a topography of emotion, at once providing a site of connection and distance.[30] Grief is also mobile in and through the body and in and through our own emotional geographies. Grief comes and goes, gets buried in a corner of our body-minds and then appears again, sometimes in moments we least expect.

Methodologically, the authors in this collection have spent their careers using qualitative, quantitative, and/or mixed methods; this breadth of methodological approaches shapes not only how they *do* their research and fieldwork but also how they are comfortable talking about it. While certain forms of methodological training may seem to lend themselves more easily to emotionally engaged, narrative reflection (e.g., ethnography or oral history methods underpinned by feminist methodologies), this collection illustrates the unique insights that researchers employing other kinds of methods (e.g., quantitative analysis, ecological surveying) contribute to an exploration of grief and witnessing in the field. Thus, it highlights and honors the different ways in which scholars and practitioners experience grief (and a wide range of other emotions) and write about those experiences; our hope is that these varied contributions speak to a wide audience of scholars, practitioners, and graduate students who engage in emotionally charged and difficult fieldwork and research.

The widely varying styles reflect not only the different disciplinary training that individual writers have received but also the ways that individuals grappled with their grappling—how they could best manage such an intimate and personal narrative within often-unforgiving professional contexts. For some of the authors in this collection, grief has been intimate and embodied—marking their affective selves with wounds of loss that cut deeply. Grappling with intimate loss in the midst of a career that rests on rigid temporal frames disallows for some kinds of mourning. Time, in some ways, becomes an enemy to the affective body, stringing along the unfinished business of grieving, erupting through the fabric of constancy and professionalism in unexpected ways and at unexpected moments.

For others in this collection, the deepest senses of grief have occurred through the act of witnessing others' pain and trauma. Some scholar-witnesses approach their research with the intent to bear witness; they anticipate and embody a politicized engagement with structural and embodied violence, often with a commitment to generating social change. Others enter their fieldwork without an intent to witness (as a political act), and an encounter or moment of coming into contact with violence and trauma radicalizes and transforms them, sometimes setting them on a different kind of path. Moving on with work and life from these encounters—the intentional or the unintentional witnessing—the scholar-witness might find themselves emotionally undone, irreparably changed; or, as Naisargi Dave writes, "something in the person ceases to exist after the event is over."[31]

But this way of thinking presumes that the witness is witnessing a finite event with a definitive beginning and end, and perhaps suggests that we are not already entangled in the structures of violence we study. Indeed, witnessing, as opposed to studying, engaging with, or looking at, requires an awareness of the depths of our multiple entanglements. It is to foreground an acknowledgment beyond subjectivity toward an intentional act of politicized embodied and affective experience. At the same time, to witness is a political act of pushing back against the invisibilization of the acts of violence against lives that are rendered ungrievable. So, too, is witnessing one's own emotional experiences pushing back against expectations of objectivity, detachment, and unemotionality in the academy, in the laboratory, at conferences, in the office. It is to honor, as Karen Barad does, the entanglements, to refuse the individuation of academia broadly and the expectations of scholarship, particularly:

> To be entangled is not simply to be intertwined with another, as in the joining of separate entities, but to lack an independent, self-contained existence. Existence is not an individual affair, individuals do not preexist their interactions. This is not to say that emergence happens once and for all, as an event or as a process that takes place according to some external measure of space and of time, but rather that time and space, like matter and meaning, come into existence, are iteratively reconfigured through each intra-action, thereby making it impossible to differentiate in any absolute sense between creation and renewal, beginning and returning, continuity and discontinuity, here and there, past and future.[32]

In some ways, then, although witnessing is neither the beginning nor the end of the work, it is the spark toward generative reimaginings of what it means to be a scholar and how to be in relation with the academy, with each other, and with our wounds. In posing the questions as we did, we invited an engagement with the visceral memories that haunt the edges of so many scholars' work, to come into their emotionality, to bear witness together—of their own bearing witness, for others to witness, to make available the witnessing of and by others.

Many of the responses to our questions about grief in the field have hinged on a politics of emotion—what is or is not allowed or acceptable as a bona fide scientist, as a visitor in the hospital, as witnesses to violence. The politics of emotion, as Sara Ahmed argues, involves "the relation between emotion and (in)justice, as a way of rethinking what it is that emotions do."[33] For many of the authors in this collection, multiple emotions underlie their work in varying ways—as experiences of personal injustice, in the witnessing of devastation, in the struggle to remain objective within the confines of academic and professional pursuits—because research does not emerge from an empty question.[34] The questions themselves arise from both curiosity and a deep investment, a sense of *caring* about and for others—others that encompass the environment, discrete ecosystems, nonhuman animals, and humans, altogether and all at once, sometimes together and sometimes as independent actors in our worldviews. In this way, grief is an embodied signifier—a driving force and an emotion that too often must be tucked away in order for researchers to be taken seriously within their fields. Indeed, the rational, distant, unemotional researcher subjectivities that so many of the authors have been trained to embody are the locus of varied fraught emotional responses.[35]

Of the many emotions that authors discuss throughout this collection, guilt and shame most commonly surface. What is it that so often manifests guilt and shame as co-occurring with grief? For some, it was the absence of grief in moments when grief would be an expected response that generated feelings of guilt. For others, it is guilt in feeling grief or shame in sharing their grief, prompting questions of who has the right to grieve and in what ways. There is also the guilt for not "doing more" or not interceding to interrupt or prevent violent encounters. And there is the shame some researchers felt in aligning themselves through inaction in complicity with those who enact violence on others.

So often, expressions of guilt and shame elicit hostility. Shame, Ahmed tells us, is "an intense and painful sensation that is bound up with how the self feels about itself, a self-feeling that is felt by and on the body."[36] This bodily felt-ness of shame is stored in the flesh as memory—reminders of an ideal social relation that, although not quite lived up to, is reaffirmed in its negation. Thus, while some may argue that guilt and shame are unproductive (and, indeed, we heard this sentiment from colleagues), we argue (and the authors insist) that these experiences tell us something important. Like anger, these emotions mark the jagged ruptures of complacency, and in their emergence they signal an intensity of interest—love, even.[37] They are not, in and of themselves, the end point but rather the starting points. These emotions and responses let us know that something is wrong; they motivate us, transform us, but they cannot be (and are not, to the authors) the transformation itself.[38]

Laughter, too, has figured prominently for some of the authors in the book. They reflect a need for laughter: the mirth and joy that laughter brings as a release, the inappropriately timed laughter that often accompanies grief, sorrow, pain, and loss, and the power of laughter to banish and transform, fleetingly, moments of great sorrow. The rawness of some of the writers' expressions—and their willingness to share these moments—reflects a vulnerability that is so often removed from the confines of academia—of its material institutions (the halls and buildings that are the campus), its professional composure (the insistence to "act like an academic"), and its refusal to acknowledge the emotionality as a site of knowledge production and theory.[39] In writing in their vulnerability, and particularly about laughter, these writers point to the ways in which emotional responses cannot be scripted, just as they cannot be tucked away, neatly packaged in a separate reality that is outside of the academy. In insisting on the outsideness of emotion, the academy, in turn, insists on the outsideness of our being. And yet, as scholars have often argued, emotion is fundamental to and deeply entangled with research (and academia broadly)—as catalyst, as response, as politics.[40]

In framing this collection, the co-occurring emotions and the stories in which they are articulated have signaled to us the emergence of a wide variety of themes and ways of understanding a complex politics of how grief manifests in the field. We realize that, by now, readers may be looking for an explanation for the ordering and themes of the chapters that follow. However, we have purposefully situated this collection as an opportunity for readers to find their own way of engaging with and understanding these stories, rather than privileging our own interpretations of what those themes might be. To that end, we have avoided providing an organizational structure that might signal hierarchies or categories of the lives and deaths we and our authors grieve. Nor did we organize the chapters by object of grief, or by levels of intimacy of grief. Instead, we've aimed to take the reader on a journey that itself is a reminder of the ways that each of us constantly moves through and across intimacies, relationalities, and caring for and about populations in our daily lives and in our broader ethical-intellectual groundings. Differences in how people mark out their personal stories throughout this collection have been left as they are to reflect the multiplicity and personal nature of affective approaches to writing.[41] The chapters are at turns surprisingly short and, at others, unexpectedly intimate, drawing the reader into a cadence that mirrors waves of grief—an uneven tempo that refuses measured engagement. They speak to each other in overlapping and dynamic ways, enlivening the possibilities for more candid dialogue across these and other frames of affective embodiment. We invite readers to generate their own interpretations and modes of building theory from these accounts, to consider the chapters in whatever order speaks to them, and perhaps, in turn, to find their own ways of articulating the many forms of grief that imbue the work we all do.

NOTES

1. Patricia J. Lopez and Kathryn Gillespie, "A Love Story: For 'Buddy System' Research in the Academy," *Gender, Place and Culture* 23, no. 12 (2016): 1689–700.

2. Kathryn Gillespie, "Witnessing Animal Others: Bearing Witness, Grief, and the Political Function of Emotion," *Hypatia* 31, no. 3 (2016): 572–88; Lopez and Gillespie, "A Love Story."

3. Kathryn Gillespie, *The Cow with Ear Tag #1389* (Chicago: University of Chicago Press, 2018).

4. James Stanescu, "Species Trouble: Judith Butler, Mourning, and the Precarious Lives of Animals," *Hypatia* 27, no. 3 (2012): 567–82; Chloë Taylor, "The Precarious Lives of Animals," *Philosophy Today* 52, no. 1 (2008): 60–72.

5. Judith Butler, *Precarious Life: The Powers of Mourning and Violence* (London: Verso, 2004).

6. Stanescu, "Species Trouble."

7. Renato Rosaldo, *Culture and Truth: Renewing the Anthropologist's Search for Meaning* (Boston: Beacon Press, 1989); Carmen Diana Deere and Diane L. Wolf, *Feminist Dilemmas in Fieldwork* (Boulder, CO: Westview

Press, 1996); Ruth Behar, *The Vulnerable Observer: Anthropology That Breaks Your Heart* (Boston: Beacon Press, 2012). See also Renato Rosaldo, Kirin Narayan, and Smadar Lavie, *Creativity/Anthropology* (Ithaca, NY: Cornell University Press, 1993); Edward J. Hedican, "Understanding Emotional Experience in Fieldwork: Responding to Grief in a Northern Aboriginal Village," *International Journal of Qualitative Methods* 5, no. 1 (2006): 17–24; Rosita Henry, "Gifts of Grief: Performative Ethnography and the Revelatory Potential of Emotion," *Qualitative Research* 12, no. 5 (2012): 528–39; Erica Southgate, "Decidedly Visceral Moments: Emotion, Embodiment and the Social Bond in Ethnographic Fieldwork," *International Journal of Work Organisation and Emotion* 4, nos. 3/4 (2011): 236–50. We are grateful to the anonymous reviewer for pointing us to these rich sources.

8. Dana Cuomo and Vanessa A. Massaro, "Boundary-Making in Feminist Research: New Methodologies for 'Intimate Insiders,'" *Gender, Place and Culture* 23, no. 1 (2016): 94–106; Alison Mountz et al., "For Slow Scholarship: A Feminist Politics of Resistance through Collective Action in the Neoliberal University," *ACME: An International E-Journal for Critical Geographies* 14, no. 4 (August 18, 2015): 1235–59.

9. Susan Guthrie et al., "Understanding Mental Health in the Research Environment," A Rapid Evidence Assessment, Royal Society and the Wellcome Trust (Cambridge, UK: RAND Europe, June 2017), https://royalsociety.org/~/media/policy/topics/diversity-in-science/understanding-mental-health-in-the-research-environm ent.pdf; Holly Else, "Academics 'Face Higher Mental Health Risk' Than Other Professions," *Times Higher Education*, August 22, 2017, https://www.timeshighereducation.com/news/academics-face-higher -mental-health-risk-than-other-professions.

10. bell hooks, *Teaching to Transgress: Education as the Practice of Freedom* (New York: Routledge, 1994), 16–17.

11. Pamela Moss and Courtney Donovan, eds., *Writing Intimacy into Feminist Geography* (London: Routledge, 2017); Danielle Drozdzewski and Dale Dominey-Howes, eds., "Researcher Trauma: Dealing with Traumatic Research Content and Places," special issue, *Emotion, Space and Society* 17 (2015); Jacque Micieli-Voutsinas and Kate Coddington, eds., "On Trauma, Geography, and Mobility: Towards Geographies of Trauma," special issue, *Emotion, Space and Society* 24 (2017).

12. Donna J. Haraway, *Primate Visions: Gender, Race, and Nature in the World of Modern Science* (New York: Routledge, 1989), 289; Gloria Anzaldúa, *Borderlands: The New Mestiza = La Frontera* (San Francisco: Spinsters/Aunt Lute, 1987); Richard Delgado, "Storytelling for Oppositionists and Others: A Plea for Narrative," *Michigan Law Review* 87, no. 8 (1989): 2411–41; Dennis Erasga, "When Story Becomes Theory: Storytelling as Sociological Theorizing," *Asia-Pacific Social Science Review* 10, no. 1 (2010): 21–38.

13. Kim V. L. England, "Getting Personal: Reflexivity, Positionality, and Feminist Research," *Professional Geographer* 46, no. 1 (1994): 80–89; Tariq Jazeel and Colin McFarlane, "The Limits of Responsibility: A Postcolonial Politics of Academic Knowledge Production," *Transactions of the Institute of British Geographers* 35, no. 1 (2010): 109–24; Linda Tuhiwai Smith, *Decolonizing Methodologies: Research and Indigenous Peoples* (London: Zed Books, 1999).

14. Victoria Lawson, "Geographies of Care and Responsibility," *Annals of the Association of American Geographers* 97, no. 1 (2007): 1–11; Doreen Massey, "Geographies of Responsibility," *Geografiska Annaler: Series B, Human Geography* 86, no. 1 (2004): 5–18; Parvati Raghuram, Clare Madge, and Pat Noxolo, "Rethinking Responsibility and Care for a Postcolonial World," *Geoforum* 40, no. 1 (January 2009): 5–13; for work on public scholarship, see Katharyne Mitchell, *Practising Public Scholarship: Experiences and Possibilities beyond the Academy* (Malden, MA; Wiley-Blackwell, 2008); Doreen Massey, "When Theory Meets Politics," *Antipode* 40, no. 3 (2008): 492–97.

15. Barbara J. King, *How Animals Grieve* (Chicago: University of Chicago Press, 2013); J. Moussaieff Masson and Susan McCarthy, *When Elephants Weep: The Emotional Lives of Animals* (New York: Delacorte Press, 1995); Connie Russell and Connie Oakley, "Engaging the Emotional Dimensions of Environmental Education," *Canadian Journal of Environmental Education* 21, no. 21 (2016): 13–22; Margo DeMello, *Mourning Animals: Rituals and Practices Surrounding Animal Death* (East Lansing: Michigan State University Press, 2016); Stanescu, "Species Trouble"; Taylor, "The Precarious Lives of Animals."

16. Paul Cloke, "Deliver Us from Evil? Prospects for Living Ethically and Acting Politically in Human Geography," *Progress in Human Geography* 26, no. 5 (2002): 587–604; David M. Smith, *Moral Geographies:*

Ethics in a World of Difference (Edinburgh: Edinburgh University Press, 2000).

17. Butler, *Precarious Life*; Judith Butler, *Frames of War: When Is Life Grievable?* (London: Verso, 2009).

18. See, for instance, bell hooks, *Feminism Is for Everybody: Passionate Politics* (Cambridge, MA: South End Press, 2000); Audre Lorde et al., *I Am Your Sister: Collected and Unpublished Writings of Audre Lorde* (Oxford: Oxford University Press, 2011); Donna McCormack, *Queer Postcolonial Narratives and the Ethics of Witnessing* (New York: Bloomsbury Academic, 2015); Kelly Oliver, "Witnessing, Recognition, and Response Ethics," *Philosophy and Rhetoric* 48, no. 4 (2015): 473–93.

19. Butler, *Precarious Life*, 33; Sara Ahmed, *The Cultural Politics of Emotion* (New York: Routledge, 2004); Kelly Oliver, *Witnessing beyond Recognition* (Minneapolis: University of Minnesota Press, 2001); Stanescu, "Species Trouble"; Taylor, "The Precarious Lives of Animals."

20. Jennifer L. Fluri and Rachel Lehr, *The Carpetbaggers of Kabul and Other American-Afghan Entanglements: Intimate Development, Geopolitics, and the Currency of Gender and Grief* (Athens: University of Georgia Press, 2017); Ahmed, *The Cultural Politics of Emotion*; Butler, *Precarious Life*.

21. McCormack, *Queer Postcolonial Narratives and the Ethics of Witnessing.*

22. The uncertainty around the time allowed for grief is further complicated by the often vague tenure expectations that are tied to a "clock" as much as the pressing global ecological and environmental emergencies and the alarming rate at which new species are declared endangered and extinct.

23. Wendy Brown, *Edgework: Critical Essays on Knowledge and Politics* (Princeton, NJ: Princeton University Press, 2005), 100.

24. Butler, *Precarious Life*, 21.

25. Inge V. del Rosario, "A Journey into Grief," *Journal of Religion and Health* 43, no. 1 (March 1, 2004): 19–28; Robert A. Neimeyer, *Techniques of Grief Therapy: Assessment and Intervention* (New York: Routledge, 2016).

26. Joyce Davidson, Liz Bondi, and Mick Smith, *Emotional Geographies* (London: Routledge, 2016); Avril Maddrell and James D. Sidaway, eds., *Deathscapes: Spaces for Death, Dying, Mourning and Remembrance* (Farnham, UK: Ashgate, 2010); Alette Willis, "Restorying the Self, Restoring Place: Healing through Grief in Everyday Places," *Emotion, Space and Society* 2, no. 2 (December 1, 2009): 86–91.

27. We follow Elizabeth Povinelli, *Economies of Abandonment: Social Belonging and Endurance in Late Liberalism* (Durham, NC: Duke University Press, 2011), in distinguishing between neoliberal governance and late liberal governmentality. By neoliberalism, we refer to the ideology, policies, and governmentality that posit the market as the single purveyor of social, political, and economic relations. See also Brown, *Edgework*; Wendy Larner, "Neo-liberalism: Policy, Ideology, Governmentality," *Studies in Political Economy*, no. 63 (Autumn 2000): 5–26. By late liberalism, we mean, explicitly, the response from within neoliberal frames to crises of legitimacy by showing "care for difference [which] is to make a space for culture to care for difference without disturbing key ways of figuring experience—ordinary habitual truths" (Povinelli, *Economies of Abandonment*, 26). In this way, late liberalism takes up projects of, and in turn formulates governance of, social difference, thereby legitimating differential belonging.

28. Avril Maddrell, "Mapping Grief: A Conceptual Framework for Understanding the Spatial Dimensions of Bereavement, Mourning and Remembrance," *Social and Cultural Geography* 17, no. 2 (2016): 166–88; Avril Maddrell, "Living with the Deceased: Absence, Presence and Absence-Presence," *Cultural Geographies* 20, no. 4 (October 1, 2013): 501–22.

29. Maddrell and Sidaway, *Deathscapes*, 3 (emphasis in original).

30. Emily Mitchell-Eaton, "Grief as Method: Topographies of Grief, Care, and Fieldwork from Northwest Arkansas to New York and the Marshall Islands," *Gender, Place and Culture*, (2019): DOI 10.1080/0966369X.2018.1553865

31. Naisargi N. Dave, "Witness: Humans, Animals, and the Politics of Becoming," *Cultural Anthropology* 29, no. 3 (2014): 440.

32. Karen Barad, *Meeting the Universe Halfway: Quantum Physics and the Entanglement of Matter and Meaning* (Durham, NC: Duke University Press, 2007), ix.

33. Ahmed, *The Cultural Politics of Emotion*, 191.

34. Kye Askins and Matej Blazek, "Feeling Our Way: Academia, Emotions and a Politics of Care," *Social and Cultural Geography* 18, no. 8 (2016): 1086–105.

35. Matthew Sparke, "Displacing the Field in Fieldwork: Masculinity, Metaphor and Space," in *Bodyspace*, ed. Nancy Duncan (London: Routledge, 1996), 212–33; Juanita Sundberg, "Masculinist

Epistemologies and the Politics of Fieldwork in Latin Americanist Geography," *Professional Geographer* 55, no. 2 (2003): 180–90.
36. Ahmed, *The Cultural Politics of Emotion*, 103.
37. See Elspeth Probyn, *Blush: Faces of Shame* (Minneapolis: University of Minnesota Press, 2005); Ahmed, *The Cultural Politics of Emotion*.
38. hooks, *Teaching to Transgress*; Angel Kyodo Owens, Lama Rod Syedullah, and Jasmine Williams, *Radical Dharma: Talking Race, Love, and Liberation.* (Berkeley: North Atlantic Books, 2016).
39. Alison M. Jaggar, "Love and Knowledge: Emotion in Feminist Epistemology," *Inquiry: An Interdisciplinary Journal of Philosophy* 32, no. 2 (1989): 151–76; Sara Ahmed, *Living a Feminist Life* (Durham, NC: Duke University Press, 2017).
40. Ahmed, *Living a Feminist Life*; Askins and Blazek, "Feeling Our Way."
41. Melissa Gregg and Gregory J. Seigworth, *The Affect Theory Reader* (Durham, NC: Duke University Press, 2011).

BIBLIOGRAPHY

Ahmed, Sara. *The Cultural Politics of Emotion.* New York: Routledge, 2004.
———. *Living a Feminist Life.* Durham, NC: Duke University Press, 2017.
Anzaldúa, Gloria. *Borderlands: The New Mestiza=La Frontera.* San Francisco: Spinsters/Aunt Lute, 1987.
Askins, Kye, and Matej Blazek. "Feeling Our Way: Academia, Emotions and a Politics of Care." *Social and Cultural Geography* 18, no. 8 (2016): 1086–105.
Barad, Karen. *Meeting the Universe Halfway: Quantum Physics and the Entanglement of Matter and Meaning.* Durham, NC: Duke University Press, 2007.
Behar, Ruth. *The Vulnerable Observer: Anthropology That Breaks Your Heart.* Boston: Beacon Press, 2012.
Brown, Wendy. *Edgework: Critical Essays on Knowledge and Politics.* Princeton, NJ: Princeton University Press, 2005.
Butler, Judith. *Frames of War: When Is Life Grievable?* London: Verso, 2009.
———. *Precarious Life: The Powers of Mourning and Violence.* London: Verso, 2004.

Cloke, Paul. "Deliver Us from Evil? Prospects for Living Ethically and Acting Politically in Human Geography." *Progress in Human Geography* 26, no. 5 (2002): 587–604.

Cuomo, Dana, and Vanessa A. Massaro. "Boundary-Making in Feminist Research: New Methodologies for 'Intimate Insiders.'" *Gender, Place and Culture* 23, no. 1 (2016): 94–106.

Dave, Naisargi N. "Witness: Humans, Animals, and the Politics of Becoming." *Cultural Anthropology* 29, no. 3 (2014): 433–56.

Davidson, Joyce, Liz Bondi, and Mick Smith. *Emotional Geographies.* New York: Routledge, 2016.

Deere, Carmen Diana, and Diane L. Wolf. *Feminist Dilemmas in Fieldwork.* Boulder, CO: Westview Press, 1996.

Delgado, Richard. "Storytelling for Oppositionists and Others: A Plea for Narrative." *Michigan Law Review* 87, no. 8 (1989): 2411–41.

DeMello, Margo. *Mourning Animals: Rituals and Practices Surrounding Animal Death.* East Lansing: Michigan State University Press, 2016.

Drozdzewski, Danielle, and Dale Dominey-Howes, eds. "Researcher Trauma: Dealing with Traumatic Research Content and Places." Special issue, *Emotion, Space and Place* 17 (2015).

Else, Holly. "Academics 'Face Higher Mental Health Risk' Than Other Professions." *Times Higher Education,* August 22, 2017. https://www.timeshighereducation.com/news/academics-face-higher-mental-health-risk-than-other-professions.

England, Kim V.L. "Getting Personal: Reflexivity, Positionality, and Feminist Research." *Professional Geographer* 46, no. 1 (1994): 80–89.

Erasga, Dennis. "When Story Becomes Theory: Storytelling as Sociological Theorizing." *Asia-Pacific Social Science Review,* 10, no. 1 (2010): 21–38.

Fluri, Jennifer L., and Rachel Lehr. *The Carpetbaggers of Kabul and Other American-Afghan Entanglements: Intimate Development, Geopolitics, and the Currency of Gender and Grief.* Athens: University of Georgia Press, 2017.

Gillespie, Kathryn. *The Cow with Ear Tag #1389.* Chicago: University of Chicago Press, 2018.

———. "Witnessing Animal Others: Bearing Witness, Grief, and the Political Function of Emotion." *Hypatia* 31, no. 3 (2016): 572–88.

Gregg, Melissa, and Gregory J. Seigworth. *The Affect Theory Reader.* Durham, NC: Duke University Press, 2011.

Guthrie, Susan, Catherine Lichten, Janna van Belle, Sarah Ball, Anna Knack, and Joanna Hofman. "Understanding Mental Health in the Research Environment." A Rapid Evidence Assessment. Royal Society and the Wellcome Trust. Cambridge, UK: RAND Europe, June 2017. https://royalsociety.org/~/media/policy/topics/diver sity-in-science/understanding-mental-health-in-the-research-en vironment.pdf.

Haraway, Donna J. *Primate Visions: Gender, Race, and Nature in the World of Modern Science.* New York: Routledge, 1989.

Hedican, Edward J. "Understanding Emotional Experience in Field-work: Responding to Grief in a Northern Aboriginal Village." *International Journal of Qualitative Methods* 5, no. 1 (2006): 17–24.

Henry, Rosita. "Gifts of Grief: Performative Ethnography and the Revelatory Potential of Emotion." *Qualitative Research* 12, no. 5 (2012): 528–39.

hooks, bell. *Feminism Is for Everybody: Passionate Politics.* Cambridge, MA: South End Press, 2000.

———. *Teaching to Transgress: Education as the Practice of Freedom.* New York: Routledge, 1994.

Jaggar, Alison M. "Love and Knowledge: Emotion in Feminist Episte-mology." *Inquiry: An Interdisciplinary Journal of Philosophy* 32, no. 2 (1989): 151–76.

Jazeel, Tariq, and Colin McFarlane. "The Limits of Responsibility: A Postcolonial Politics of Academic Knowledge Production." *Trans-actions of the Institute of British Geographers* 35, no. 1 (2010): 109–24.

King, Barbara J. *How Animals Grieve.* Chicago: University of Chicago Press, 2013.

Larner, Wendy. "Neo-liberalism: Policy, Ideology, Governmentality." *Studies in Political Economy,* no. 63 (Autumn 2000): 5–26.

Lawson, Victoria. "Geographies of Care and Responsibility." *Annals of the Association of American Geographers* 97, no. 1 (2007): 1–11.

Lopez, Patricia J., and Kathryn Gillespie. "A Love Story: For 'Buddy System' Research in the Academy." *Gender, Place and Culture* 23, no. 12 (2016): 1689–700.

Lorde, Audre, Rudolph P. Byrd, Johnnetta Betsch Cole, and Beverly Guy-Sheftall. *I Am Your Sister: Collected and Unpublished Writings of Audre Lorde.* Oxford: Oxford University Press, 2011.

Maddrell, Avril. "Living with the Deceased: Absence, Presence and Absence-Presence." *Cultural Geographies* 20, no. 4 (October 1, 2013): 501–22.

———. "Mapping Grief: A Conceptual Framework for Understanding the Spatial Dimensions of Bereavement, Mourning and Remembrance." *Social and Cultural Geography* 17, no. 2 (2016): 166–88.

Maddrell, Avril, and James D. Sidaway, eds. *Deathscapes: Spaces for Death, Dying, Mourning and Remembrance.* Farnham, UK: Ashgate, 2010.

Massey, Doreen. "Geographies of Responsibility." *Geografiska Annaler: Series B, Human Geography* 86, no. 1 (2004): 5–18.

———. "When Theory Meets Politics." *Antipode* 40, no. 3 (2008): 492–97.

Masson, J. Moussaieff, and Susan McCarthy. *When Elephants Weep: The Emotional Lives of Animals.* New York: Delacorte Press, 1995.

McCormack, Donna. *Queer Postcolonial Narratives and the Ethics of Witnessing.* New York: Bloomsbury Academic, 2015.

Micieli-Voutsinas, Jacque, and Kate Coddington. "On Trauma, Geography, and Mobility: Towards Geographies of Trauma." Special issue, *Emotion, Space and Place* 24 (2017).

Mitchell, Katharyne. *Practising Public Scholarship: Experiences and Possibilities beyond the Academy.* Malden, MA: Wiley-Blackwell, 2008.

Mitchell-Eaton, Emily. "Grief as Method: Topographies of Grief, Care, and Fieldwork from Northwest Arkansas to New York and the Marshall Islands." *Gender, Place and Culture,* (2019): DOI 10.1080/0966369X.2018.1553865

Moss, Pamela, and Courtney Donovan, eds. *Writing Intimacy into Feminist Geography.* London: Routledge, 2017.

Mountz, Alison, Anne Bonds, Becky Mansfield, Jenna Loyd, Jennifer Hyndman, Margaret Walton-Roberts, Ranu Basu, Risa Whitson, Roberta Hawkins, Trina Hamilton, and Winifred Curran. "For Slow Scholarship: A Feminist Politics of Resistance through Collective Action in the Neoliberal University." *ACME: An International E-Journal for Critical Geographies* 14, no. 4 (August 18, 2015): 1235–59.

Neimeyer, Robert A. *Techniques of Grief Therapy: Assessment and Intervention.* New York: Routledge, 2016.

Oliver, Kelly. *Witnessing Beyond Recognition.* Minneapolis: University of Minnesota Press, 2001.

———. "Witnessing, Recognition, and Response Ethics." *Philosophy and Rhetoric* 48, no. 4 (2015): 473–93.

Owens, Angel Kyodo, Lama Rod Syedullah, and Jasmine Williams. *Radical Dharma: Talking Race, Love, and Liberation.* Berkeley: North Atlantic Books, 2016.

Povinelli, Elizabeth. *Economies of Abandonment: Social Belonging and Endurance in Late Liberalism.* Durham, NC: Duke University Press, 2011.

Probyn, Elspeth. *Blush: Faces of Shame.* Minneapolis: University of Minnesota Press, 2005.

Raghuram, Parvati, Clare Madge, and Pat Noxolo. "Rethinking Responsibility and Care for a Postcolonial World." *Geoforum* 40, no. 1 (January 2009): 5–13.

Rosaldo, Renato. *Culture and Truth: Renewing the Anthropologist's Search for Meaning.* Boston: Beacon Press, 1989.

Rosaldo, Renato, Kirin Narayan, and Smadar Lavie. *Creativity/Anthropology.* Ithaca, NY: Cornell University Press, 1993.

Rosario, Inge V. del. "A Journey into Grief." *Journal of Religion and Health* 43, no. 1 (March 1, 2004): 19–28.

Russell, Connie, and Connie Oakley. "Engaging the Emotional Dimensions of Environmental Education." *Canadian Journal of Environmental Education* 21, no. 21 (2016): 13–22.

Smith, David M. *Moral Geographies: Ethics in a World of Difference.* Edinburgh: Edinburgh University Press, 2000.

Smith, Linda Tuhiwai. *Decolonizing Methodologies: Research and Indigenous Peoples.* London: Zed Books, 1999.

Southgate, Erica. "Decidedly Visceral Moments: Emotion, Embodiment and the Social Bond in Ethnographic Fieldwork." *International Journal of Work Organisation and Emotion* 4, nos. 3/4 (2011): 236–50.

Sparke, Matthew. "Displacing the Field in Fieldwork: Masculinity, Metaphor and Space." In *Bodyspace*, edited by Nancy Duncan, 212–33. London: Routledge, 1996.

Stanescu, James. "Species Trouble: Judith Butler, Mourning, and the Precarious Lives of Animals." *Hypatia* 27, no. 3 (2012): 567–82.

Sundberg, Juanita. "Masculinist Epistemologies and the Politics of Fieldwork in Latin Americanist Geography." *Professional Geographer* 55, no. 2 (2003): 180–90.

Taylor, Chloë. "The Precarious Lives of Animals." *Philosophy Today* 52, no. 1 (2008): 60–72.

Willis, Alette. "Restorying the Self, Restoring Place: Healing through Grief in Everyday Places." *Emotion, Space and Society* 2, no. 2 (December 1, 2009): 86–91.

CHAPTER ONE

"With You, Time Flowed Like Water"

Geographies of Grief across International Research Collaborations

JESSIE HANNA CLARK

> It's not as if an "I" exists independently over here and then simply loses a "you" over there, especially if the attachment to "you" is part of what composes who "I" am. If I lose you, under these conditions, then I not only mourn the loss, but I become inscrutable to myself. Who "am" I, without you?[1]

When I left after my first summer of master's research in 2006 in Diyarbakır, Zeynep scribbled her contact information in my field book, neither of us knowing when I would be back.[2] Underneath her address she wrote, "*seninle zaman su gibi akiyordu*" (with you, time flowed like water).[3] That summer, we walked kilometers of Diyarbakır's oldest streets, home at that time to thousands of displaced families, on a quest to understand what a more urban, postconflict, and still deeply poor Kurdistan looked like in Turkey. Our friendship began as part of a three-month thesis project and turned into eleven years of dissertation and postdissertation research together. Again and again we returned to these same streets by foot to visit friends. Since summer 2015 and a violent renewal of conflict between the Kurdistan Workers' Party (PKK) and the Turkish state in urban centers in Eastern Turkey, however, time has not flowed like water; rather, time together is fleeting, broken, and uncertain. My regular and reliable visits to Diyarbakır and Zeynep's periodic visits to the United States are now as unpredictable as the political climate in Turkey. Even electronic communication is uncertain. During the state of emergency first implemented in the southeast region in 2015 and throughout Turkey in 2016, our daily communication over WhatsApp was interrupted for hours and sometimes days at a time due to state-sanctioned regional internet outages. The political transformations unfolding in Turkey, especially in Kurdish southeast Turkey, over the last two years have halted our ability to work together, transformed (and destroyed) the neighborhoods where we once worked, and brought into stark relief both the precarity existing in our relationship across vastly uneven political and economic conditions and the fundamental precariousness of our two lives now bound together as colleagues and friends.

OUR DISPOSSESSED LIVES

Precarity and precariousness, two distinct concepts for Judith Butler, might be best understood through the term *dispossession*, a follow-up theme that Butler and Athena Athanasiou explore in a series of dialogues recorded in 2013. To be dispossessed "refers to processes and ideologies by which persons are disowned and abjected by normative and normalizing powers that define cultural intelligibility and that regulate the distribution of vulnerability."[4] *Precarity*, then, describes the politically induced condition of being outside "norms of recognition" that cast certain lives as unlivable and, therefore, ungrievable.[5] During the most intense periods of urban violence that beset cities in southeast Turkey in 2015–16, for example, the contours of human life were drawn in international and Turkish media to frame Kurdish lives, especially young Kurds' lives, as unlivable—as "terrorists."[6] A common refrain heard in Diyarbakır refers back to a set of instructions given to Turkish soldiers in the early years of the Turkish Republic as they were tasked with suppressing any Kurdish resistance. The word *Kürt*, the soldier's service manual said, referred to the sound the snow makes when you step on it.[7] The neighborhoods that flared up in conflict in summer 2015 in southeastern cities echoed the proverbial crunch of snow that has come to define life for many Kurds under the Turkish Republic, including Zeynep.

Butler and Athanasiou describe dispossession in a second way, as that which "encompasses the constituted, preemptive losses that condition one's being dispossessed by another: one is moved to the other and by the other—exposed to and affected by the other's vulnerability."[8] In this sense, precariousness requires a recognition of the ontological human condition in which all life inherently and necessarily exists in relationships of dependence and vulnerability. In *Frames of War*, Butler specifically focuses on the experience of grief as a foundational moment in the understanding that "one's life is always in some sense in the hands of the other."[9] In my case, I apprehended the precarious nature of my own life when I confronted deep loss and the possibility of loss beginning in 2014. In the United

States, my mother was rediagnosed with cancer, a fight she ultimately lost in December 2016. In that time and since I continue to be haunted by one question: *Who am I without you?* Simultaneously, in summer 2015, the neighborhoods where Zeynep and I spent months and years listening to people's stories became the stage for fighting between a youth wing of the PKK and the Turkish military. The violence led to the mass displacement of families, several thousand deaths, and the destruction of physical communities. During this time, I would wait for a response over WhatsApp for an indication that Zeynep and her family were OK. The same question returned again: *Who am I without you?* My sense of self as a researcher, a teacher, a human is profoundly intertwined with my life in Diyarbakır, the sisterhood and familyhood that I entered into in 2006. My sense of self was upended in 2015 and 2016 as two pivots of stability and security spun out, faster together, probably, than apart.

Butler writes: "When we lose some of these ties by which we are constituted, we do not know who we are or what to do. On one level, I think I have lost 'you' only to discover that 'I' have gone missing as well. At another level, perhaps what I have lost 'in' you, that for which I have no ready vocabulary, is a relationality that is composed neither exclusively of myself nor you, but is to be conceived as the tie by which those terms are differentiated and related."[10] The ethics of precarious life calls us to recognize the deep ways we are constituted by and within others; this, in turn, requires that people and places cast outside "norms of recognition" be apprehended not according to an externally defined set of principles or rights but to the survival and wellness of one's own and every being. What follows is a testament to my friendship with Zeynep that explores the precarious life of our now eleven-year research collaboration. I asked Zeynep if she would like to coauthor this chapter with me. She declined. She was able to read a copy, though. My intention in this piece was not to speak for Zeynep. In addition to trying to convey as much from my own perspective as possible, my words echo many conversations that Zeynep and I have had together. Our plan is to publish together freely one day and for her, especially, to share her stories of Diyarbakır.

SUMMER 2006-SUMMER 2015

I returned to Diyarbakır a week before the June 7 Turkish general elections in 2015 to begin a period of reconnaissance work for a new project with Zeynep. The trip marked nine years and seven trips since we met in April 2006, when Zeynep appeared in the lobby of my guesthouse one evening after I had spent a long day searching for a female translator. She was also a graduate student and was learning English, and we were keen to put our respective language skills (my Turkish and Kurdish, her English) to the test—however unsuccessfully we might. She gathered my items and immediately marched me to the home she shared with her mother, father, and four siblings. As Zeynep says, I "never left." What began as translation services turned into an intimate research partnership. Since 2006, Zeynep has become a best friend, a sister, and, we joke, my "partner in crime." In the time leading up to 2015, we passed two comprehensive exams; wrote and defended two master's theses and one doctoral dissertation; participated in two international conferences together, one in Diyarbakır and one in Seattle during Zeynep's first visit to the United States; and greatly improved our language skills.

Our research examines questions around women and development in Diyarbakır's poorest neighborhoods. The research, like our friendship, was formed and nurtured over long conversations tracing and retracing our steps through Diyarbakır's many "back streets." It was here that we marveled at the *kader* (fate) that brought us together. This routinely included lamenting the "normal path" that we did not take as women in our respective cultures and musing on the people we would have been had we not met ("boring," I say; "married, most likely," Zeynep laughs, turns up her nose, and adds, "with five children"). We also talked about who we are for meeting. I remember our walk home together after one interview in Diyarbakır in spring 2009, when Zeynep told me that she was reconnecting with a past she had altogether buried in the wake of gunshots in the street and fears of walking to school in the mid-1990s at the peak of PKK-state conflict. Hearing stories of resilience from women who escaped to the city and raised families as single mothers made her proud because this was also her story as a Kurdish woman. I lived with Zeynep's family for most of the research, sitting out on the balcony during the summer late at night eating sunflower seeds, drinking tea, discussing our interviews, sharing stories of old Diyarbakır and hopes for political futures near and far that seemed more achievable when we were together.

In early 2010, at the start of our dissertation research, Zeynep's father passed away. I sat by her and her family in their grief. I had never lost a parent. At thirty, Zeynep had lost two, her father and her second mother. While open mourning—crying, yelling, moaning—is an appropriate and almost expected response among women during the weeklong Muslim burial process, I observed how grief transformed into a more solitary and private affair in the weeks and months that followed. I shared this time of isolation with Zeynep, and it was on our journeys to the neighborhoods to work that we shared stories of her father. To honor her father and his kindness in welcoming me into his family, my parents and I traveled to Diyarbakır for Zeynep's brother's wedding in 2012. When my mother was diagnosed with late-stage cancer in fall 2014, my relationship with Zeynep and her family and the beliefs and rituals around death in predominantly Muslim Diyarbakır allowed me to navigate grief in meaningful ways. After my mother passed, Zeynep's brother, the new patriarch still thirty years junior to my father, would call over WhatsApp every several days to order my father to leave the house and take a walk. "It is healthy. We will all be together soon ... *inshallah*," he said, as he imagined out loud his mother and father, now passed, sharing a cup of tea with my mother. The shared grief of losing a parent is one of many experiences on which our work together is built, especially in the environments where we work, where loss is a regular part of everyday life. These moments together in grief, joy, and contemplation, mapped across many years now, have inextricably linked Zeynep's fate to mine as researchers and as friends, fostering an ethical responsibility not only to each other and our families but also to the vastly different places we are from. Butler writes, "To be injured means that one has the chance to reflect upon injury, to find out the mechanism of its distribution, to find out who else suffers from permeable borders, unexpected violence, dispossession, and fear and in what ways."[11] The injury that loss (or the prospect of loss) inevitably imposes upon the self exposes the raw vulnerability that binds all beings together. To see and feel that fragility of self is both a terrible and a beautiful process that nurtures an understanding and a curiosity of the nature of others' suffering and especially its connection to one's own.

SPRING 2015–SPRING 2017

When I arrived in the earliest days of June 2015, Diyarbakır was singing. After decades of PKK-Turkish conflict, a pro-Kurdish party was positioned to achieve parliamentary representation for the first time in history and a two-year peace process was under way. Diyarbakır is popularly referred to by some Kurds as the "unofficial capital of Kurdistan" and has long been a focal point for Turkish and Kurdish ethnic and nationalist anxieties. In recent years, a continued and important need to memorialize the past had been overwhelmed by a stronger desire to position the city as a voice for peace and multiculturalism in the future. It was these motives that drove families, young giggling girls, and old men and women to the train station to support a new era in Turkish-Kurdish relations, embodied visually in the large Turkish flags floating alongside the Peoples' Democratic Party flags below the main stage. Zeynep and I were also there that day. In our years of overly cautious and thoughtful work together, it was the first time we had ever ventured to a political meeting, a testament to the sense of peace we felt.

The peace—or hope for peace, at least—that afternoon was short-lived. In the early moments of the rally, two bombs were detonated, allegedly by ISIS (although some accuse the Justice and Development Party administration), killing four and wounding two hundred. The pro-Kurdish party would go on to win a historic number of votes and secure parliamentary representation for the first time in history. Four months later, however, a second election would return single-party power to President Erdogan's Justice and Development Party, a victory fashioned, in part, through a campaign of fear around Kurdish "terrorism." The bomb on that sunny July afternoon was a symbolic and literal declaration for a new period in Turkish history, one that has severely limited the ability of many Turkish citizens, and especially Kurdish citizens, to live and work freely. As is often the case, the names and photos of the victims were nearly impossible to find in the media coverage of the aftermath. This invisibility at the national level was echoed in the months that followed in international media coverage. In the month following the July general elections, a Kurdish youth movement organizing since 2013, the Patriotic Revolutionary Youth Movement (YDG-H), took up arms against the Turkish state and declared neighborhoods in cities across the southeast autonomous—including two of the neighborhoods where Zeynep and I worked in Diyarbakır. Turkish security forces responded with heavy military force. Today, those two neighborhoods are gone. We knew many families who were uprooted. We knew several children who had joined the YDG-H.

In the days after the rally, Zeynep and I cried and laughed. Humor has carried us through a lot in the course of our friendship, particularly in the tensest moments. Zeynep would laugh with her friends and family retelling the story of me interrupting her shower, fearful of a rhythmic booming coming from outside. The evening of the attack, as word spread across the city, residents came to their windows to flicker apartment lights and bang pots and pans to contest the violence and honor those who had died. When I finally understood what was happening, we too joined in the chorus of mourning, flipping the light switch on and off, on and off. It was healing. We also joked about what the headlines in the US newspapers would say if the two of us had been hurt or worse: "One American, and a few others injured," we imagined. The unevenness of our political and economic positions is often the butt of our jokes. I returned to the

United States three weeks later and have not returned to Diyarbakır since.

My grief for the loss of these neighborhoods is also and always intertwined with my grief for my friend. In the following years since that summer, various opposition and activist efforts have been quashed, particularly after the attempted coup in summer 2016. Zeynep visited Reno again that winter. On the other end of her WhatsApp calls home, her mother would quiet any political talk in case someone was listening. We have been careful to limit our conversations to secure lines, such as encrypted WhatsApp, but our conversations are still self-censored. Zeynep was generous enough to FaceTime my introductory human geography class to talk about the role of Kurdish language in her identity, but I was careful to divert any questions from students that were overtly political. Some, but not all, could appreciate the enormity and privilege of her virtual presence in our classroom. I am aware that as a Kurd and a Turkish citizen, her role in our research—and her voice and image on the other end of the computer and phone—is infinitely more dangerous than mine. While I have always had the privilege to leave the field, and to write and speak freely about our research, she cannot. Safety, rather than collaboration, now shapes the priorities of our work. And safety means silence, a silence that permeates national and international coverage of conflict in Kurdish Turkey and a silence that also lingers in the figurative seat that my "partner in crime" occupies next to me.

BECOMING "UNDONE"

At the end of my first summer working in Diyarbakır, en route back to the United States, I read Jhumpa Lahiri's collection of short stories, *Interpreter of Maladies*. On the back page of my field notebook from 2006, not many pages from Zeynep's address, I wrote a passage from the story "The Third and Final Continent": "As strange as it seemed, I knew in my heart that one day her death would affect me, and, stranger still, that mine would affect her."[12] Lahiri's words convey the reality of close and sustained field relationships and aptly describe life's dependent and always precarious condition. I knew when I met Zeynep that our relationship would be more than a summer fling of research—that, in fact, our friendship would become ingrained in who I am and how I would tell stories about the places I research. We are inherently vulnerable for the fact that our existence as human beings is tied to the existence of others. That vulnerability is entrenched in research: the storytellers we become, the professions built on these stories, and our own well-being are dependent on both the voices *and* the well-being of others. As researchers, we are marked with what Emmanuel Levinas calls "traces" of Others, of the presence of all those whom we work with and the places we work within.[13] In this relational ontology, there is potential for political transformation, when we see and communicate other places as wholly human and interconnected to our own *precarious lives*. Despite current political dangers, and the uneven *precarity* they highlight, we accomplish necessary social and political work in these relationships. We become better researchers and better people. "Let's face it," Butler says. "We're undone by each other. And, if we're not, something's missing."[14]

NOTES

1. Judith Butler, *Precarious Life: The Powers of Mourning and Violence* (London: Verso, 2004), 22.

2. I would like to thank Zeynep. *Seninle su gibi akıyordu.*

3. All names in this chapter are pseudonyms.

4. Judith Butler and Athena Athanasiou, *Dispossession: The Performative in the Political* (Cambridge: Polity Press, 2013), 2.

5. Butler and Athanasiou, *Dispossession*, 2.

6. Butler and Athanasiou, *Dispossession*, 2.

7. *Kurd* in Turkish is spelled *Kürt.* Nicole Pope and Hugh Pope, *Turkey Unveiled: Atatürk and After* (London: John Murray, 1997), 251–52.

8. Butler and Athanasiou, *Dispossession*, 1.

9. Judith Butler, *Frames of War: When Is Life Grievable?* (London: Verso, 2009), 14

10. Butler, *Precarious Life*, 22.

11. Butler, *Precarious Life*, xii.

12. Jhumpa Lahiri, *Interpreter of Maladies* (New York: Mariner Books, 2003).

13. Emmanuel Levinas, *Humanism of the Other* (Chicago: University of Illinois Press, 2006).

14. Butler, *Precarious Life*, 23.

BIBLIOGRAPHY

Butler, Judith. *Frames of War: When Is Life Grievable?* London: Verso, 2009.

———. *Precarious Life: The Powers of Mourning and Violence.* London: Verso, 2004.

Butler, Judith, and Athena Athanasiou, *Dispossession: The Performative in the Political.* Cambridge: Polity Press, 2013.

Lahiri, Jhumpa. *Interpreter of Maladies.* New York: Mariner Books, 2003.

Levinas, Emmanuel. *Humanism of the Other.* Chicago: University of Illinois Press, 2006.

Pope, Nicole, and Hugh Pope. *Turkey Unveiled: Atatürk and After.* London: John Murray, 1997.

CHAPTER TWO

Grieving Guinea Pigs

Reflections on Research and Shame in Peru

MARÍA ELENA GARCÍA

ENCOUNTERING GUINEA PIGS

It was a sweltering day in February 2012 when Walter picked me up at my grandmother's apartment in Lima, Peru. Walter was taking me to his guinea pig farm, located about two hours north of Lima.[1] The farm was new—just a few months in the making. Walter had almost eight thousand *reproductoras*, or female guinea pig breeders, at another farm, but people had broken in and destroyed that facility.[2] "They left several hundred dead ones," he told me angrily, "and they left me lots of dead babies." He was quiet for several minutes. But then he added with a smile that he was resilient and determined to get his business back on track. He was struggling financially, but he was convinced of the productive value of this business, and excited about the possibilities guinea pig production offered.

We arrived at Walter's farm at around three in the afternoon. The sun was strong and the air was thick. I was seven months pregnant at the time, and in the stifling heat and humidity of this Lima summer, I was miserable. My feet and hands were swollen and sore, my throat cried out for constant hydration, and my back was in pain with the weight of this new life in me. Maybe it was the physical discomfort, or the dryness of my throat, or the hyperawareness of life at that moment that made it so difficult to look at the fourteen hundred or so guinea pigs at Walter's farm that day. The guinea pigs were divided between two *galpones*, a Spanish word that connotes a kind of warehouse of life where one could store plants, animals, or, in a different historical moment, slaves. These galpones were made of corrugated tin, each with a double ceiling designed to help keep the heat at bay.

As soon as we entered I heard guinea pigs scurrying; their high-pitched squealing piercing the air; all of them scrambling to the same corner of their respective enclosures, clustering together in fear and becoming a single mass. Most of the large and round guinea pigs in the enclosure were female, and most had just given birth, or were about to give birth.[3] At first glance, the animals looked fine—healthier and more alert than I thought would be the case given the stifling heat. But I noticed that the galpones did not include any water for the animals. When I asked about this, Walter told me the animals got all the water they needed from the *forraje*, the roughage they ate.[4] I expressed my worry that what was left of the forraje in each of the dozens of enclosures seemed dry because of the heat, and he suggested we give them more. Walter took an armful of the rough branches leaning against the walls of the galpón and handed them to me. The branches were heavy and jagged, and they scratched my arms as I tried to place them gently on the ground around the guinea pigs, so as not to startle or hit the animals. I watched as Walter threw the branches at them, quickly and roughly. He laughed at my technique, saying that the way I was laying down the roughage would take all day and that there was no need to be so careful.

As I placed the forraje in each pen and looked more closely at the animals, I caught other details. One mother who had just given birth was repeatedly nudging a dead baby, eventually giving up and moving on to clean the three others around her. Another round guinea pig was lying on her side, not moving much, and not looking well. I called Walter over. He looked at her, nodded, and said she was most likely dying of birthing complications. He leaned over, squeezed her, moved her around. She barely responded. So, Walter picked her up and roughly tossed this pregnant, dying guinea pig out of the cage onto the dirt floor behind us. "She is almost gone. She will be dead by morning if not sooner," he said, placing a hand on my back and moving me away from that cage and toward another larger pen with dozens of very young guinea pigs huddling close together in the corner.

CULINARY REVOLUTIONS AND THE
GUINEA PIG IN PERU

Over the past decade, Peru has undergone what many term a "gastronomic revolution."[5] Peruvian cuisine is arguably the most significant source of pride for Peruvians today, and the single most important dimension of a national campaign for the global marketing and branding of the country.[6] My current work explores the biopolitics of culinary nationalism: thinking about how bodies are produced, managed, and consumed, for whom, and to what end. I have been particularly struck by the postcolonial aesthetics of this moment, as the success of Peruvian gastronomy depends on what has been described as a "beautiful fusion" of ingredients—on the celebration of Peru's particular mixture of race, culture, and history.[7] This mostly translates into the appropriation of Native ingredients (e.g., quinoa, alpaca, guinea pig) to authenticate a *Peruvian* fusion cuisine. It also promises to erase histories of racial inequalities by supporting the Native producers of these products and incorporating them into the national culinary movement. Elsewhere I develop a critique of this celebratory narrative and complicate the hegemonic claim that this gastronomic boom promotes social inclusion. On the contrary, this new celebration and consumption of Peruvian high cuisine remains firmly anchored in elite spaces and perpetuates settler-colonial violence and hierarchies.[8] But in this essay, I want to reflect on the place guinea pigs occupy in this gastronomic revolution.

Guinea pigs, animals used for food in Peru, play a significant role in this new moment, especially as an authentically Peruvian animal commodified as the key ingredient that helps to anchor and indigenize "sophisticated" expressions of Andean cuisine. For centuries, the *cuy* (as the guinea pig is known in the Andes) has played a central role in the culinary and spiritual lives of Andean peoples. For this very reason, the cuy is associated with indigeneity; in other words, the animal is associated with poverty and "backwardness." In the last fifteen years, however, emerging networks of tourism, development, and cuisine have generated a rediscovery of the cuy. Indeed, a guinea pig boom (*boom del cuy*) has accompanied the culinary revolution in Peru. Today there are dozens of courses and workshops that provide training for those interested in becoming cuy producers on a small, medium, or large scale. This growing demand for cuyes has led to new development and commercial schemes for extracting greater economic gains from cuy production and reproduction.

Walter is the head of Super Cuy, a private guinea pig production company based in Lima. And he is very much a part of Peru's gastronomic revolution and the narratives of economic success that accompany it. His passion used to be focused on the large-scale export of guinea pigs to the United States, but today he is quite intensely (and almost exclusively) involved in the national promotion of cuy.[9] Through his business, he offers online courses about cuy production for Peruvians at home and abroad; he organizes conferences of cuy producers and cuy culinary and cultural festivals. And he owns a cuy breeder farm located just north of Lima. Walter believes in the boom del cuy. His family has lived on the margins of Lima's sprawling metropolis for years, but through his business ("thanks to the cuy," he says), he is slowly inching his way in. But Walter's gratitude is more specific than this. His most valuable assets are the female bodies of the thousands of guinea pigs he owns. Over lunch before arriving at his farm, he talked for quite some time about his reproductoras, emphasizing that he earns at least three times as much from one breeder than from selling a male or a "spent" female cuy for meat. "I care for them deeply. I love my little ladies" (*Les tengo mucho cariño. Quiero mucho a mis mujercitas*), he told me. I was struck particularly by the language of love and care, seamlessly woven within a narrative of love and profit.

SHAME AND RESEARCH

Anthropologist Naisargi Dave reminds us that "love is an injustice because when we love it is the one or ones who are special to us that we save."[10] Going back to my encounter with the pregnant guinea pigs at Walter's farm, I am reminded that what I saw as an abyss between my pregnancy (full of futurity, love, and possibility) and theirs (all about profit and marked for certain death) was in itself problematic. Although I am hesitant to say that my physiological status as a pregnant woman provided understandings that are unavailable to others who are not pregnant (or who are not women), there was indeed something—a somatic specificity perhaps—that opened up a space for me to connect with those pregnant animals; it allowed me to see them, or perhaps to feel them, in ways that might not have been possible or available to me if I had not also been carrying another life inside of me. Thinking about the pregnant cuy dying of birthing complications, tossed aside onto the dirt floor to die, at that moment, I tried not to betray my sadness. I tried to disconnect myself from Walter's roughness. I tried not to think about the cuy's wounded body, now lying alone, in the dusty, sweltering heat. And for the first time in my anthropological career, I felt shame. Of course, anthropology, with its colonial legacies, offers us much to be ashamed about. But my own positioning has meant that from the time I began my anthropological training, I have been aware of this dark past, and as a woman of color, as an anthropologist committed to decolonizing and collaborative engaged research, I have always felt confident in my place within and even against the discipline.

Going back to that dying cuy, I'm not sure what I could have done differently in that moment. I'm not sure that anything would have changed had I done more than simply continue to walk, more than allow Walter to move me away from her. But I am compelled to theorize that moment of shame—the shame of taking *his* side; of worrying about *my* research, about what would happen if I criticized his actions. Would doors close? Would my concern for this cuy raise questions about my work that might imperil access to these kinds of spaces? Would it raise questions about my motivation for conducting this research? Alice Kuzniar's work on melancholia comes to mind here, as she explores what happens when "affective feelings [for the animal] are disavowed and when the identification with [the animal] becomes the object of shame."[11] What does it mean for an ethnographer, I would add, when identification with the animal becomes the object of suspicion?

In Peru, my interest in cuyes—in other-than-human life—is often read as an interest in gastronomy or development, in the role these animals play in ideas of national progress and the global commodification of Peru. Among some of my Peruvian colleagues this interest is also read as a concern over the place of guinea pigs in racial representations and as figures of colonial legacies. But considering the lives of guinea pigs—worrying about control over their bodies and beings, about the production of animal life in the service of global capitalism—is seen by many of my Peruvian interlocutors as at best laughable, and at worst a form of violence in and of itself. Given the pervasive animalization of Indigenous Peruvians, and the use of animal rights campaigns to disparage particular cultural traditions, I understand why so many friends and colleagues link animal "rights" talk or simply concern over the lives of animals to authoritarian and racist ideologies and practices. In this context, how can we worry about nonhuman life in the midst of crushing human poverty? How do we insist on the intimate and entangled histories of race and species, on the unpredictable linkages between human and nonhuman suffering? Can this project challenge both anthropocentric *and* settler-colonial narratives?

I found myself thinking about ethnography as betrayal as I reflected on this research trip. It became clear to me, in the moment of walking away from the dying cuy, that my project, the so-called multispecies research I was conducting, was taking place at the expense of the animal. After visiting the breeder farm, during the drive back to my grandmother's apartment, Walter had invited me to participate in a cuy production workshop he was offering the weekend following my departure. My first response to his invitation was a deep feeling of regret. Why couldn't I stay longer in Lima? Should I change my flight so that I could attend the workshop? This would certainly not be the last time Walter offered this kind of workshop, but the urge to be as "efficient" and "productive" as I could in that moment of fieldwork (before my baby was born) was powerful. As I thought more about what participant observation might mean in this context, however, I began to worry. Walter had walked me through the different parts of the workshop. As a workshop participant, you learn how to pick the best "specimens." You learn to weigh them, what to feed them, how to house them. You also learn how to kill. And you practice by trying out several different kill methods that include breaking the neck, slicing the throat while holding the animal, slicing the throat while the animal hangs upside down in a steel cone, and stunning before scalding to death.[12] I had already been a party to this violence by eating the guinea pigs that Walter served me before visiting his farm. But would I be capable of doing the killing? And even if I chose not to participate but simply observed instead, would I be able to witness the suffering of so many animals being killed by unskilled hands? Or was this line of inquiry, my assumptions and presumptions about suffering and killing, foreclosing epistemological possibilities?

CONCLUDING THOUGHTS

As a Peruvian woman and anthropologist, I have found it a challenge to think about these difficult questions for multiple reasons. But the concerns I explore here—the questions I am grappling with about care and killing, life and death, race and settler colonialism, poverty and the nonhuman, and my own positionality as a Peruvian anthropologist based in the United States, committed to collaborative and decolonial frameworks—also pose a profound personal and intellectual challenge because they take me back to my grandmother. My grandmother was the person who taught me so much in her kitchen. She was a woman who knew how to kill chickens and guinea pigs to feed her family when she lived in rural Peru but who more recently enjoyed the convenience of supermarkets and delivery chicken in her home in urban Lima. As the smells and memories of my grandmother's kitchen became entangled with increasingly violent forms of industrial agriculture, I found myself wondering about the dark sides of love and the slow death that seems to envelop us all.

Scholars in multiple fields are worrying with increasing specificity about how to apprehend ethnographically the vital presence of nonhuman actors. But I want to focus on the problem, and on the contradictions, of multispecies ethnographic work. Multispecies research, if taken to mean that nonhuman lives matter beyond metaphor and symbolism, raises new questions about the intersection of ethics and methods. Is killing other-than-human animals an acceptable dimension of participant observation? Is eating them during field research? And is observing their dying bodies, moving past them, and doing nothing in the moment, also acceptable? The ethnographic emphasis on, and methodological imperative of, nuance, complexity, and contradiction has meant that we are too often bracketing or betraying the animal. In this kind of work, human engagements displace nonhuman ones. To enter Walter's farm, I must be Walter's friend, not the guinea pigs.' To understand the fate of the guinea pigs, I cannot save them.

But maybe there is some hope that can be found in the echoes of these moments. In writing about the ethnographic encounter as one of tragedy and loss, I hope to open up the productive possibilities that come with mourning and grieving. As I try to make some sense of how my encounters in Peru could speak broadly to the emerging anthropologies of nonhuman life, perhaps the clearest lesson emerges around the powerful experience of shame. Other scholars in the field of animal studies note the powerful and jarring experience of coming face-to-face with cruelties that we can only observe and document but not prevent. Kathryn Gillespie describes the shame she felt in the course of her ethnographic research on cow auctions. She recounts one image in particular in which a day-old calf, torn away from his mother and standing alone in the openness of the auction yard, searches for comfort by nuzzling the leg of an auctioneer only to receive a smacking blow from the paddle in his hand.[13] Gillespie's eyes, wide with shock, were noticed by the man, who looked straight at her, then began to laugh nervously. Gillespie, in a swirl of methodological worry, nervousness, and dismay, could only force herself to smile uneasily in return. It is a reaction that haunts her.

In his affecting memoir *Eating Animals*, Jonathan Safran Foer explores this terrain of shame. He expands on Walter Benjamin's and Franz Kafka's reflections on the link between eating animals, shame, and forgetting. He says: "Shame is the work of memory against forgetting. Shame is what we feel when we almost entirely—yet not entirely—forget social expectations and our obligations to others in favor of our immediate gratification."[14] He continues: "Silently the animal catches our glance. The animal looks at us, and whether we look away ... or not, we are exposed. Whether we change our lives or do nothing, we have responded. To do nothing is to do something."[15]

What I want to propose here is that multispecies ethnographic research is necessarily, if only partially, an engagement with shame and against forgetting. But reflecting on this research, writing and producing multispecies ethnographies, can be a way to remember, a way to conjure up the shame of the ethnographic encounter as a pathway toward recalling and challenging violence. It can be a way to grieve for the other-than-human beings included in our work. Centering grief and rage as methodological inspiration and practice is not new in anthropological writing.[16] But it has thus far been primarily a human-centered endeavor. The recent anthropological turn to multispecies ethnography is an important corrective to this. Writing about the violence done to guinea pig bodies *as violence*, for instance, is a way to "do something," to grieve, to remember.

At their best, multispecies ethnography and animal studies can help us move from what Claire Jean Kim calls the politics of disavowal to an ethics of avowal.[17] For my own work in Peru, I think back to the pregnant guinea pig Walter said would not survive her birthing complications and who was tossed onto the dirt, to die alone and forgotten. Writing about her and remembering her is perhaps a small gesture, but it is one way, the only way I have now, to refuse the idea that her life does not count, that hers is not a grievable life.

NOTES

1. I have used pseudonyms throughout this essay to protect the privacy of those mentioned here.

2. Walter did not know who broke into his farm, but he suspected it was young men also looking to open their own production business and wanting to avoid having to pay for starter guinea pigs.

3. Each enclosure included approximately seven female guinea pigs and one male guinea pig, in addition to any babies recently born.

4. Since this visit, Walter has changed his approach and now offers water to his pregnant guinea pigs. When I asked him about this change, he told me that giving them water helps avoid maternal death and improves the percentage of infant survival. This, he told me, is good for business.

5. See Judith Fan, "Can Ideas about Food Inspire Real Social Change? The Case of Peruvian Gastronomy," *Gastronomica* 13, no. 2 (2013): 29–40; María Elena García, "Culinary Fusion and Colonialism: A Critical Look at the Peruvian Food Boom," *ReVista: Harvard Review of Latin America*, Fall 2014, http://revista.drclas.harvard.edu/book /culinary-fusion-and-colonialism; and Raúl Matta, "República gastronómica y país de cocineros: Comida, política, medios y una nueva idea de nación para el Perú," *Revista Colombiana de Antropología* 50, no. 2 (2014): 15–40.

6. See more on Marca Perú (or PerúTM) at http://internacional .peru.info/es/home. One particularly striking campaign involved the "invasion" of Peru, Nebraska: http://www.youtube.com/watch?v=r_x BZcVEHiI.

7. See Gastón Acurio, *Sazón en Acción: Algunas recetas para el Perú que queremos* (Lima: Aerolíneas Editoriales, Mitin, 2016); Gastón Acurio, *Peru: The Cookbook* (London: Phaidon Press, 2015); and Simeon Tegel, "Peru's Fantastic Food Revolution," *The Guardian*, September 21, 2012.

8. See María Elena García, "The Taste of Conquest: Colonialism, Cosmopolitics, and the Dark Side of Peru's Gastronomic Boom," *Journal of Latin American and Caribbean Anthropology* 18, no. 3 (2013): 505–24.

9. Walter worked tirelessly to establish a national holiday for the cuy. In 2013, the Ministry of Agriculture declared the National Day of the Guinea Pig, a holiday to be celebrated yearly every second Friday

in October. The goal is to promote and increase guinea pig consumption in the country and abroad.

10. Naisargi Dave, "Love and Other Injustices: On Indifference to Difference," Franklin Humanities Institute, Duke University (2016), https://humanitiesfutures.org/papers/845/.

11. Alice Kuzniar, *Melancholia's Dog: Reflections of Our Animal Kinship* (Chicago: University of Chicago Press, 2006).

12. Walter lamented that due to lack of space and technological capacity, he could not include a fifth method: electrocution. The larger farms in Ecuador and southern Peru, he told me, no longer need to employ people because they are mechanizing death much like in the North. According to Walter, in those slaughter facilities guinea pigs are placed on a thin layer of water and electrocuted before being scalded.

13. Kathryn Gillespie, *The Cow with Ear Tag #1389* (Chicago: University of Chicago Press, 2018).

14. Jonathan Safran Foer, *Eating Animals* (New York: Back Bay Books, 2009), 37.

15. Foer, *Eating Animals*, 38.

16. Renato Rosaldo, *The Day of Shelly's Death: The Poetry and Ethnography of Grief* (Durham, NC: Duke University Press, 2013).

17. Claire Jean Kim, *Dangerous Crossings: Race, Species and Nature in a Multicultural Age* (Cambridge: Cambridge University Press, 2015).

BIBLIOGRAPHY

Acurio, Gastón. *Peru: The Cookbook*. London: Phaidon Press, 2015.

———. *Sazón en Acción: Algunas recetas para el Perú que queremos*. Lima: Aerolíneas Editoriales, Mitin, 2016.

Dave, Naisargi. "Love and Other Injustices: On Indifference to Difference." Franklin Humanities Institute, Duke University, 2016. https://humanitiesfutures.org/papers/845/.

Fan, Judith. "Can Ideas about Food Inspire Real Social Change? The Case of Peruvian Gastronomy." *Gastronomica* 13, no. 2 (2013): 29–40.

Foer, Jonathan Safran. *Eating Animals*. New York: Back Bay Books, 2009.

García, María Elena. "Culinary Fusion and Colonialism: A Critical Look at the Peruvian Food Boom." *ReVista: Harvard Review of Latin America*, Fall 2014. http://revista.drclas.harvard.edu/book/culinary-fusion-and-colonialism.

———. "The Taste of Conquest: Colonialism, Cosmopolitics, and the Dark Side of Peru's Gastronomic Boom." *Journal of Latin American and Caribbean Anthropology* 18, no. 3 (2013): 505–24.

Gillespie, Kathryn. *The Cow with Ear Tag #1389.* Chicago: University of Chicago Press, 2018.

Kim, Claire Jean. *Dangerous Crossings: Race, Species and Nature in a Multicultural Age.* Cambridge: Cambridge University Press, 2015.

Kuzniar, Alice. *Melancholia's Dog: Reflections of our Animal Kinship.* Chicago: University of Chicago Press, 2006.

Matta, Raúl. "República gastronómica y país de cocineros: Comida, política, medios y una nueva idea de nación para el Perú." *Revista Colombiana de Antropología* 50, no. 2 (2014): 15–40.

Rosaldo, Renato. *The Day of Shelly's Death: The Poetry and Ethnography of Grief.* Durham, NC: Duke University Press, 2013.

Tegel, Simeon. "Peru's Fantastic Food Revolution." *The Guardian*, September 21, 2012. https://www.theguardian.com/travel/2012/sep/21/peru-lima-food-restaurants-revolution.

CHAPTER THREE

An Immigrant in Academia

Navigating Grief and Privilege

YOLANDA VALENCIA

Being in between the margins and academia is a site of grief; it is
a space where theory and empirics meet. Academia and my
immigrant world are both my communities and my fields, and I
grieve in both. I often contemplate what happens when a person
who meets the criteria of the "other" (here referred to as immigrants of color; more specifically, Mexican immigrants) inhabits
academia, when the "other" is at times considered part of "us,"
and when the witness relates to the witnessed (or is the same).
Although I now have access to the privileged world of academia,
I continue to consider myself a Mexican immigrant who—along
with my immigrant community—has been placed in the category of the "other," the disposable, the ungrievable. It is my goal
to write by and for my immigrant community, to write our own
stories in ways that empower our community and help us build
and strengthen our third consciousness and the consciousness of
those who are willing to listen. And yet, as I outline here, this
work comes with its own complexities. I draw on my own experiences witnessing and experiencing cultural and material dis-

possession and displacement in Mexico, as well as labor exploitation, suffering, and injustice in the United States to frame my discomfort with and grief about my shifting positionality. It is this insightful experience that makes me feel both anger and love and gives me strength to uncover the "unseen."

BECOMING AN IMMIGRANT

When I was growing up in Mexico, the price of corn—a main crop my family cultivated—was falling in relation to other products; jobs grew scarcer, and the cost of living continued to increase. As early as I can remember, my father would migrate to the United States as an undocumented worker, each time promising it would be his last trip. However, that was never the case—within a few months of his return from a two-year journey, rushed plans to migrate to the United States would begin once again. In order to keep his employment, my father was expected to return to the United States within a set period of time. In response to my mother's insistence to bring us with him, my father would explain that crossing *por el cerro* (through the mountains) was extremely dangerous; that he would never take us to El Norte without papers as we could die in our attempt to cross. And yet, he himself tasted the flavor of death every time he crossed the US-Mexico border—or the "Devil's Highway," as Luis Alberto Urrea calls it—as an undocumented migrant seeking work in the US agricultural sector, leaving his own small agricultural community and family behind for years.[1] He did so in order to provide for us—his children and family.[2] Paradoxically, this resulted in our growing up without a father, and my mother raised the five of us by herself. It was difficult for my father to send remittances because he needed to save to pay back my aunt who resided in the United States and always loaned him money to pay for his expensive trip—including for the coyote (a guide to cross the border). He also needed to pay for his daily living expenses. Meanwhile, in Mexico, from a very young age, my four older siblings and I helped our mother by working in the informal economy: selling food in the market, bus station, and streets.

My family's experiences reflect the level of intimacy in which big-P politics—including (1) transnational trade policies that created unfair competition from highly subsidized US crops, (2) immigration laws that produce the "illegal," and (3) militarization of the US-Mexico border that forces people to risk their lives to cross it—interact with people's lives and produce traumatizing experiences for people of all ages and their families. While my father obtained residency as a result of the Immigration Reform and Control Act (IRCA) of 1986, it wasn't until I was seventeen years old that he was able to *arreglarnos papeles* (get us documents) and bring us to the United States in the mid-1990s. Only the two youngest children qualified. My older siblings had to stay behind. To keep our residency, we were expected to live in the United States for at least six months each year. It was not possible, though, for us to live in the United States for part of the year and return to Mexico, since it was too expensive to pay for our US apartment year-round. As a result, we stayed in the United States permanently. If my siblings wanted to come and reunite with us, they would have to risk their lives at the militarized border, and if they survived, they would be considered "illegal aliens" here in the United States. Further, their options for employment would be limited to racialized exploitative labor in food processing plants, service, or the agricultural sector— just as opportunities for my father were for many years and as the employment options for eleven million undocumented people continue to be. Within this context, I consider myself an immigrant whose family transcends—but is also divided by—national borders; an immigrant who has been intimately affected by historical and contemporary national and transnational policies both in Mexico and in the United States.

My story is one of many. In Mexico, more than 50 percent of the population have at least one relative who has been forced to migrate to the United States in search of safety, to reunite with their family, and/or to find their lost job—mainly lost as a result of unfair trade policies.[3] Obtaining a permit to enter the United States with documents is almost impossible for displaced migrants because one of the requirements is proof of wealth. Obtaining refugee status is a long and risky process; often, people fleeing violence do not have the luxury of waiting for a decision to be made, and worse, such requests are frequently denied. Thus, just like my father and many members of my community, every year thousands taste death at the militarized US-Mexico border, where hundreds die and no one is held responsible for such deaths.[4] On the contrary, our participation—as US citizens and (in)direct supporters of unfair policies—in making other places unlivable, and in sponsoring border building and increased militarization resulting in an increasingly deadly buffer zone, tends to be blurred and distorted via neoliberal discourses of individualism, self-responsibility, choice, and un/deservingness.[5] Their lives (our lives) as they cross the militarized border are devalued to the point of not deserving protection or justice on either side of the border. Crossing this buffer zone, *por el cerro*, is like crossing a deadly space of limbo where a person loses legal existence and protection but cannot escape the law's punishment as they are often arrested and experience expedited removal or languish in jail for weeks or even months. Sadly, this phenomenon is worsening, as militarization and closure of the border increase—especially after the September 11, 2001, terror attacks—with the excuse of protecting "us" (US citizens) from "them" (immigrants of color, potential "terrorists"). My origins and painful experiences across borders—Mexico, the United States, my immigrant community, and academia—determine a large part of who I am: what, how, and from where I see, question, write, think, process, and so forth. This is why my research always considers places of origin and experiences across national and local boundaries and seeks to uncover material consequences of historical processes across space. More important, it seeks to politicize inequality, suffering, and unequal distribution of life chances.

IMMIGRANT AND UNDERGRAD: ON WHAT I COULD NOT SAY

Soon after arriving in the United States, and after overcoming a series of obstacles, I attended a community college and then transferred to Eastern Washington University to earn a BA in finance and economics. I wanted to be employable. There, I was often the only person of color in my classes. Sometimes the students and teacher would discuss how immigrants supposedly take advantage of the system, do not pay taxes, and damage "our" economy. I wanted to speak up but could not: my English was broken, I did not have "objective" proof to say the opposite, and I felt alone and unsupported. My body shook, my hands sweated, and my heart raced, but I never managed to say anything.

I would recall how, soon after arriving in the United States, in order to help our father pay for our costly trip, my sister, mother, and I were forced to do farm labor for my father's longtime employer, and how we worked in food processing plants and in the slaughterhouse because employers at other local businesses denied our applications since, they said, we could not speak English or did not have previous work experience. Doing farm labor was enormously difficult, but working in the slaughterhouse was by far the worst job I have ever done. In all these jobs, I met many people with different migration status. We all worked extremely hard for minimum wage; we all paid taxes and contributed exactly the same through automatic withholdings from our paychecks—real or fake Social Security numbers, it did not matter—before it got to our hands. The difference was (and is) that those with documentation were eligible for benefits, including unemployment when laid off and Social Security pension when retired. People without documents were not. Thus, undocumented people not only contribute to the economy but also subsidize the cost of everyone's food by working for low wages and also subsidize the social safety net even as they are prevented from obtaining benefits. Denial of such benefits is often taken as a normal consequence for making a "rational choice" to migrate without documentation. The impossibility of getting documentation and the frustration that comes with it, and also the hope for a comprehensive immigration reform with every presidential election, are constant and almost palpable in my immigrant community. The last immigration reform took place more than thirty years ago—in 1986—and so this hope was met again and again with disappointment. I knew all this. I experienced it myself in an intimate and painful manner. I grew up without a father and worked in the informal economy in Mexico from a very young age. My family was forced to migrate to the United States, and I was constrained to racialized, exploitative labor on my arrival here. I am part of the immigrant community who continues to experience this every day, and yet, the lump in my throat did not allow me to speak up in those college classrooms. Although I was a student and part of the student body and community, and thus part of the "us" at that moment, I also felt excluded and like I was in the wrong place.

ACADEMIA: MY FIELDWORK

Rooted in this personal history, when I was presented with the opportunity to attend graduate school, my priority was to study economics in order to reveal how immigrants contribute positively to the economy of the United States. Within the schools to which I applied, none of the professors in the economics departments worked on topics related to immigration; most were creating models and formulas to figure out how to make the most profits out of businesses. It was with enormous gratitude and hope that I joined the geography department at the University of Washington. The department provided me with enormous intellectual growth, support, and motivation. It is here that I gained academic knowledge and expanded my consciousness. Reading articles and books that uncover the political dimensions of inequality and unequal distribution of life chances filled my eyes with tears. I finally saw how the situation of my community in Mexico and in the United States related to the theories and historical processes I was studying.

It was here, in the university, that I explored and learned about the power of discourse to justify laws that produce and reinforce distribution of unequal life chances, exclusion, othering, and criminality.[6] Learning this was painful but also powerful as I also realized the importance of my immigrant community's agency, courage, unity, and love in producing thriving spaces under conditions set for our failure.[7] This awareness is what I wish to share with my community, but it has taken me years of intense academic study to come to this understanding. Unfortunately, this is a luxury that most in my immigrant community do not have because they are forced to do backbreaking racialized work for miserable wages, and those made *undocumented* by law face further barriers. Such reality is often erased/ignored/forgotten in academic settings. In academia, most of my students and peers are whites, whereas in agricultural and factory labor, almost all the workers are Latinxs—mostly undocumented Mexican immigrants. Sadly, the elimination of the Deferred Action for Childhood Arrivals (DACA) policy in September 2017 put eight hundred thousand youth and families at risk of deportation and farther away from reaching an opportunity for academic careers and access to such powerful knowledge, keeping the academy as a white and elite place, and white supremacy stronger than ever.[8]

PAINFUL ABSENCES IN ACADEMIC CONFERENCES

During the 2016 annual meeting of the American Association of Geographers, I attended a wonderful plenary talk. The speaker argued that analyses of racial genealogies uncover how historical racial processes are tied to *current racism*. The talk focused on the Great Migration, when millions of African Americans migrated north to escape the horrible working conditions of the agrarian sector, in turn, triggering an attempt by southern landowners to keep African Americans in place by offering various "benefits." As the speaker discussed the importance of agricultural work in US wealth accumulation and empire building, I thought about my father, who migrated as undocumented—risking his life at the border—to do agricultural labor. I also thought of my extensive immigrant community that continues to work in the fields of Washington State in terrible conditions for miserable wages. The speaker referred to that era as one of premechanization of agriculture and did not mention current agrarian workers. Had I not known that agriculture still needs a lot of human labor—and that this labor is highly racialized, dangerous, exploitative, and low-waged—I would have assumed that machines now cultivate all of our fruits and vegetables. This talk, as great as it was, made me feel erased. I felt the absence of my immigrant community in this conversation; our situation is so relevant to the topic, and yet there was no mention of it at all. And while I understand that contemporary agricultural labor was not the focus of the talk, it is the absence of deeper conversations about race and white supremacy that is frustrating. The commentary in response to this talk was inspirational. The commentator mentioned the important role of the US-Mexico war in US imperial expansion: more land required more labor. She also mentioned how capitalism is always racist—it constantly seeks cheap labor and thus has taken advantage of different populations, including poor whites. There I could see a small glimpse of my immigrant community. While I was trying to thank the commentator for her words after the session, tears streamed down my cheeks and prevented me from saying anything. As I reflected on this experience, I realized that my identity is primarily as a Mexican immigrant, an immigrant in academia who constantly ties what she reads, hears, and learns with her immigrant community.

·   ·   ·

Being in between the margins and academia is a site of grief; it is a space where theory and empirics meet. Academia and my immigrant world are both my communities and my fields, and I grieve in both. In my immigrant world, it is devastating to see policies displacing populations and laws damaging my immigrant community being enacted while programs—such as DACA—that benefit some members of this community are eliminated. All of these actions are justified with negative discourses that frame immigrants as the "other" (mainly Mexicans and immigrants of color) while framing the "us" (mainly those of European descent and white supremacists) as legitimate citizens deserving of protection. In academia: while gaining knowledge and connecting theory and historical processes to my immigrant community's situation is powerful, it is also painful. Noticing the absence of my immigrant community, both physically and in intellectual academic discussions, is upsetting. This is why I write by and for my immigrant community. I connect historical processes with detrimental situations in places of origin and in the United States to denormalize white supremacy and politicize policies enacted against immigrants of color, to politicize inequality, and to challenge negative discourses and the laws that are justified by them. I join those scholars who write from the margin, for whom the *testimonios* of the oppressed are theoretical knowledge, who wish to remove the slash in *nos/ otras*—where *nos* means *us* and *otras* means "others," but without the slash it simply means "us."[9] No, we are not criminals or terrorists, we do not steal jobs, we do not take advantage of the system. We are your neighbors, your friends, your coworkers, your classmates, your peers. This is not to devalue other people by implying that we are not what others could be, as Lisa Marie Cacho cautions us.[10] Rather, I seek to increase consciousness about our common planetary humanity and dependent interconnection. As Arturo Escobar says, "People and communities have the right to be different precisely because 'we' are all *equals!*"[11]

ACKNOWLEDGMENTS

My most profound appreciation to the editors of this book, Kathryn Gillespie and Patricia J. Lopez, for their significant contributions, support, and friendship. Special thanks to my mentor, Victoria Lawson, for her priceless and ongoing support. My deepest gratitude to my beautiful daughters and caring husband for their patience and love. From the bottom of my heart, I thank my mother for raising five children mainly on her own: *Gracias mamá—te quiero mucho!*

NOTES

1. Luis Alberto Urrea, *The Devil's Highway: A True Story* (New York: Little, Brown, 2004).

2. Deborah A. Boehm, "'For My Children': Constructing Family and Navigating the State in the US-Mexico Transnation," *Anthropological Quarterly* 81, no. 4 (2008): 777–802.

3. On searching for safety, see Dawn Paley, *Drug War Capitalism* (Oakland, CA: AK Press, 2015); on family reunification, see Deborah A. Boehm, "US-Mexico Mixed Migration in an Age of Deportation: An Inquiry into the Transnational Circulation of Violence," *Refugee Survey Quarterly* 30, no. 1 (March 1, 2011): 1–21; on the search for work, see Matthew Sparke, *Introducing Globalization: Ties, Tensions, and Uneven Integration* (Chichester: Wiley-Blackwell, 2013); Joseph Nevins, "Dying for a Cup of Coffee? Migrant Deaths in the US-Mexico Border Region in a Neoliberal Age," *Geopolitics* 12, no. 2 (March 14, 2007): 228–47; on the impact of uneven trade policies, see Jennifer Clapp, *Food* (Malden, MA: Polity Press, 2012).

4. Nevins, "Dying for a Cup of Coffee?"; Urrea, *The Devil's Highway*; Oscar Martínez, *The Beast: Riding the Rails and Dodging Narcos on the*

Migrant Trail, trans. Daniela Maria Ugaz and John Washington (repr., London: Verso, 2014).

5. Alexandria J. Innes, "International Migration as Criminal Behaviour: Shifting Responsibility to the Migrant in Mexico-US Border Crossings," *Global Society* 27, no. 2 (2013): 237–60.

6. Lisa Marie Cacho, *Social Death: Racialized Rightlessness and the Criminalization of the Unprotected* (New York: New York University Press, 2012); Dean Spade, *Normal Life: Administrative Violence, Critical Trans Politics, and the Limits of Law* (Brooklyn, NY: South End Press, 2011); Leo R. Chavez, *The Latino Threat: Constructing Immigrants, Citizens, and the Nation* (Palo Alto, CA: Stanford University Press, 2013).

7. Katherine McKittrick and Clyde Adrian Woods, *Black Geographies and the Politics of Place* (Toronto: Between the Lines, 2007).

8. While imperfect and exclusionary, DACA—created by Obama—provided some undocumented youth protection from deportation, employment authorization (through work permits), and eligibility for driver's license. On the whiteness of academia, see Audrey Kobayashi, Victoria Lawson, and Rickie Sanders, "A Commentary on the Whitening of the Public University: The Context for Diversifying Geography," *Professional Geographer* 66, no. 2 (May 2014): 230–35.

9. bell hooks, *Feminist Theory from Margin to Center* (Boston: South End Press, 1984); Minerva S. Chávez, "Autoethnography, a Chicana's Methodological Research Tool: The Role of Storytelling for Those Who Have No Choice but to Do Critical Race Theory," *Equity and Excellence in Education* 45, no. 2 (April 1, 2012): 334–48; John Beverley, "The Margin at the Center: On *Testimonio* (Testimonial Narrative)," *Modern Fiction Studies* 35, no. 1 (1989): 11–28; The Latina Feminist Group, *Telling to Live: Latina Feminist Testimonios* (Durham, NC: Duke University Press, 2001); Dolores Delgado Bernal, Rebeca Burciaga, and Judith Flores Carmona, "Chicana/Latina Testimonios: Mapping the Methodological, Pedagogical, and Political," *Equity and Excellence in Education* 45, no. 3 (July 2012): 363–72; Rachel Silvey and Victoria Lawson, "Placing the Migrant," *Annals of the Association of American Geographers* 89, no. 1 (March 1999): 121; Gloria Anzaldúa, *Light in the Dark/Luz en lo oscuro: Rewriting Identity, Spirituality, Reality*, Latin America Otherwise (Durham, NC: Duke University Press, 2015); Sofia A. Villenas, "AESA 2012 Presidential Address: 'What My Community Means to Me':

Reimagining Civic Praxis with Latina/Chicana Feminisms," *Educational Studies* 51, no. 1 (January 2, 2015): 72–84.

10. Cacho, *Social Death*.

11. Arturo Escobar, "Worlds and Knowledges Otherwise," *Cultural Studies* 21, no. 2–3 (March 1, 2007): 188 (emphasis added).

BIBLIOGRAPHY

Anzaldúa, Gloria. *Light in the Dark/Luz en lo oscuro: Rewriting Identity, Spirituality, Reality*. Latin America Otherwise. Durham, NC: Duke University Press, 2015.

Beverley, John. "The Margin at the Center: On *Testimonio* (Testimonial Narrative)." *Modern Fiction Studies* 35, no. 1 (1989): 11–28.

Boehm, Deborah A. "'For My Children': Constructing Family and Navigating the State in the US-Mexico Transnation." *Anthropological Quarterly* 81, no. 4 (2008): 777–802.

———. "US-Mexico Mixed Migration in an Age of Deportation: An Inquiry into the Transnational Circulation of Violence." *Refugee Survey Quarterly* 30, no. 1 (2011): 1–21.

Cacho, Lisa Marie. *Social Death: Racialized Rightlessness and the Criminalization of the Unprotected*. New York: New York University Press, 2012.

Chavez, Leo R. *The Latino Threat: Constructing Immigrants, Citizens, and the Nation*. Stanford, CA: Stanford University Press, 2013.

Chávez, Minerva S. "Autoethnography, a Chicana's Methodological Research Tool: The Role of Storytelling for Those Who Have No Choice but to Do Critical Race Theory." *Equity and Excellence in Education* 45, no. 2 (2012): 334–48.

Clapp, Jennifer. *Food*. Malden, MA: Polity Press, 2012.

Delgado Bernal, Dolores, Rebeca Burciaga, and Judith Flores Carmona. "Chicana/Latina *Testimonios*: Mapping the Methodological, Pedagogical, and Political." *Equity and Excellence in Education* 45, no. 3 (2012): 363–72.

Escobar, Arturo. "Worlds and Knowledges Otherwise." *Cultural Studies* 21, no. 2 (2007): 179–210.

hooks, bell. *Feminist Theory from Margin to Center.* Boston: South End Press, 1984.

Innes, Alexandria J. "International Migration as Criminal Behaviour: Shifting Responsibility to the Migrant in Mexico-US Border Crossings." *Global Society* 27, no. 2 (2013): 237–60.

Kobayashi, Audrey, Victoria Lawson, and Rickie Sanders. "A Commentary on the Whitening of the Public University: The Context for Diversifying Geography." *Professional Geographer* 66, no. 2 (2014): 230–35.

The Latina Feminist Group. *Telling to Live: Latina Feminist* Testimonios. Durham, NC: Duke University Press, 2001.

Martínez, Oscar. *The Beast: Riding the Rails and Dodging* Narcos *on the Migrant Trail.* Translated by Daniela Maria Ugaz and John Washington. Reprint, London: Verso, 2014.

McKittrick, Katherine, and Clyde Adrian Woods. *Black Geographies and the Politics of Place.* Toronto: Between the Lines, 2007.

Nevins, Joseph. "Dying for a Cup of Coffee? Migrant Deaths in the US-Mexico Border Region in a Neoliberal Age." *Geopolitics* 12, no. 2 (2007): 228–47.

Paley, Dawn. *Drug War Capitalism.* Edinburgh: AK Press, 2015.

Silvey, Rachel, and Victoria Lawson. "Placing the Migrant." *Annals of the Association of American Geographers* 89, no. 1 (1999): 121.

Spade, Dean. *Normal Life: Administrative Violence, Critical Trans Politics, and the Limits of Law.* Brooklyn, NY: South End Press, 2011.

Sparke, Matthew. *Introducing Globalization: Ties, Tensions, and Uneven Integration.* Chichester: Wiley-Blackwell, 2013.

Urrea, Luis Alberto. *The Devil's Highway: A True Story.* New York: Little, Brown, 2004.

Villenas, Sofia A. "AESA 2012 Presidential Address 'What My Community Means to Me': Reimagining Civic Praxis with Latina/Chicana Feminisms." *Educational Studies* 51, no. 1 (January 2, 2015): 72–84.

CHAPTER FOUR

The Mongoose Trap

Grief, Intervention, and the Impossibility
of Professional Detachment

ELAN ABRELL

I have always been an animal lover.[1] I was the kind of kid who would watch *Mutual of Omaha's Wild Kingdom* and get upset that the person filming a lion hunting a gazelle did not drop the camera and save the gazelle. At the time, I was too young to understand the complicated issues tied up in debates over the ethics of intervention and documentation, such as those that arose in response to photojournalist Kevin Carter's (in)famous photograph of a young, emaciated Sudanese girl crouched in the dust as a vulture stalked her from behind, waiting for her to expire.[2] The experience of watching a gazelle die on television may have been my first exposure to the idea that grief over the death of another being can be a powerful impetus to action, even if the only action I could take at the time was to express my frustration that there was nothing else I could do.

Decades later, while conducting ethnographic research on US animal sanctuaries, I repeatedly and unexpectedly found myself thinking of Carter's haunting photo as my experiences of grief for some of the animals I encountered undermined my efforts to maintain what my formalized academic training taught me should be "objective" professional detachment from my research subjects. An effort at such detachment seemed especially important since I supported the missions of the organizations where I engaged in participant observation. Out of a desire to understand the values and motivations of the sanctuary caregivers I encountered, I endeavored to approach my research with a level of objectivity that would at least enable me to avoid conflating my own ethical commitments with those of my human interlocutors. As it turned out, the diverse views of the caregivers I encountered made the risk of conflation less of an issue than I thought it would be. In fact, the biggest challenges to preserving a degree of objective detachment arose when our perspectives seemed to differ the most, especially in situations involving life-or-death decisions about other animals. In these moments, I struggled to determine my own moral responsibilities as a witness to suffering and death that I had the ability to prevent, albeit at the cost of collapsing the critical distance I tried to preserve as a researcher. Focusing on a particular experience from my fieldwork involving a troubling encounter with a mongoose, I examine how attempting to resolve the dilemma of either abandoning my aspiration to critical distance or ignoring grief's impetus to action helped me to reconcile this tension between observation and intervention.

Anybody who has spent significant time at an animal sanctuary can tell you that animal suffering and death are all too common phenomena. Animals often come to sanctuaries with injuries or illnesses that can cause early death or chronic pain that, in worst-case scenarios, may lead to euthanasia. But there are also other kinds of animal death in sanctuaries. In facilities that care for carnivores, for example, other animals need to be killed (either on the sanctuary premises or somewhere else) for sanctuary carnivores to survive. Many sanctuaries must also contend with external predators that pose a danger to the animals in their care. Some employ nonlethal strategies to protect their animals from predators, but as I learned through my research, others include lethal methods in their "predator control plans."

One of my field sites, an exotic animal sanctuary in Hawai'i called Rainbow Haven, occasionally has problems with mongooses.[3] Mongooses are cat-sized mammalian carnivores that look similar to their relative, the meerkat, and were introduced to Hawai'i in 1883 by sugar plantation owners in the hopes that they would help control the growing rat population. Rats—now framed as an "invasive species"—came to the islands by boat much earlier, accompanying the archipelago's original Polynesian settlers as well as later European explorers.[4] However, in what has now become a familiar tale of the ways in which the elimination of so-called invasive species frequently backfires, the introduction of mongooses did not have the desired effect. While rats are nocturnal, mongooses are diurnal. Rather than forming a predator-prey dynamic that could rid the islands of rats and save native bird species from their predation, rats and mongooses together made bird hunting a twenty-four-hour affair, with rats on the night shift and mongooses on the day shift.

Shortly before I arrived at Rainbow Haven in the summer of 2013, a mongoose sneaked into an area at the sanctuary that caregivers called "The Lagoon"—a small fenced-in area with a pond. Several different waterfowl lived there, including a gray crowned crane named King, three nenes (a vulnerable species of goose native to the Hawaiian Islands), a duck named Dewey, and

Billie the swan. Most of these birds were injured in the wild and brought to the sanctuary by concerned humans. Caregivers nursed them back to health, but none of the birds could be rehabilitated enough to be released safely back to the wild. The mongoose had killed a duck named Huey, leaving Dewey alone as the sole duck in The Lagoon.

Olivia, the founder of the sanctuary, explained to me that because Rainbow Haven has a permit for endangered species rehabilitation (of which the nenes are beneficiaries), the state requires the facility to have a plan in place to protect its animals from predators. While at the time of this writing "invasive species" is not a regulatory category in Hawai'i (as it is under federal law), the nonnative mongoose is classified as "injurious wildlife," a regulatory designation applied to "any species … which is known to be harmful to agriculture, aquaculture, indigenous wildlife or plants, or constitute a nuisance or health hazard."[5] As such, mongooses have historically been subjected to population management efforts that include trapping and killing or the use of a poison called diphacinone.[6] Further, because mongooses are "injurious wildlife," such killing is allowed under the state's animal cruelty laws.[7] Given their legal status, Olivia saw killing mongooses as the most efficient way to protect sanctuary animals from their predation. The sanctuary's regime of care and violence and its differential impact on various animals emerged out of the intersection of legal and ecological frameworks of value that render animals like mongooses killable and animals like nenes in need of saving.

The procedure for dealing with mongooses in the plan was simple: set a trap for them and kill any who were caught in the trap. A sanctuary intern named Seth explained to me, "When Olivia finds out there's a mongoose in the trap, she gets a gun and shoots it in the head and throws the body over the fence." On one of my first days at the sanctuary, I accompanied Seth and Olivia to bait the mongoose trap with dry cat food. The "live trap" was a rectangular cage with an open end. When an animal enters the cage to get the bait at the closed end, their weight on a platform in the middle causes a door on the open end to close behind them. The bait is placed near the closed end of the trap so that an animal must enter the cage and stand on the platform to eat it. The trap was not unfailing; an animal had managed to steal the bait the day before without getting caught. Olivia showed us how to set the trap properly and put more food in for bait. As she did this, she explained a disturbing idiosyncrasy about how the trap worked with mongooses: "When you shoot a mongoose in the trap, you don't need any more bait for awhile after that. Mongooses live in family units of parents and offspring. The blood from the first kill will attract the other family members night after night until they are all dead." I was not sure how accurate this was, but I felt an anger-tinged sorrow at the self-compounding injustice of the deadly chain reaction that would ensnare multiple mongooses, possibly by exploiting their own concern for fellow mongooses. I said nothing, though, trying just to observe and listen while pushing my own feelings to the back of my mind.

The next morning, as I was feeding breakfast to the birds in The Lagoon, I saw a movement in the trap outside the fence. A dirty-blonde mongoose was pacing in tight circles inside the rusty, long, shoebox-shaped cage. I froze, not knowing what to do. For a moment, I considered telling Seth and Olivia they had caught a mongoose. Prior to coming to this sanctuary, I assumed that I would never intentionally participate in or facilitate the killing of another animal (except for possibly euthanizing one who was suffering and otherwise untreatable) and that I would try to intervene if I ever saw somebody else attempting to hurt or kill an animal. This simplistic assumption did not, however, account for the complexity of situations in which it may be required to weigh the value of one life against another. Since arriving at the sanctuary, I had already been confronted with such a dilemma and failed to intervene as I silently observed one of the interns kill mice to feed several sanctuary raptors. Watching her snap the necks of small mice with a quick pinch of her fingers, I felt queasy and cold. Striving to maintain a critical detachment as both observer and researcher from what I was witnessing so that I could understand how *she* felt about her killing of certain animals in the care of others, I endeavored to suspend my own desire to ask her to stop (or even just to walk away to avoid witnessing the killing) by partially rationalizing her actions to myself as necessary for the raptors' survival.

The idea of killing the mongoose in the cage felt harder to rationalize. Her death was not necessary for the sustenance of other animals. She did pose a potential threat to the birds in The Lagoon, but that was only a possibility, not an inevitability. And while I understood how the lives of sanctuary animals are not only valued above those of external predators by caregivers but legally privileged over the lives of "injurious wildlife" by the state, I did not personally share this view. Most important, though, the mice killing did not require my cooperation. Telling the others about the mongoose would make me a direct participant in her eventual death. I considered just continuing with the morning feedings without reporting the mongoose's entrapment, but somebody else would eventually find her. By not saying anything, I would only postpone her death. Nonetheless, I found myself trying to again rationalize nonintervention, wondering if the mongoose was responsible for Huey's death. Had she already acted "injuriously," and if so, could that help constrain my affective engagement with these circumstances to that of the professional observer? Even if she had, I did not actually think that this justified killing her. Further, the purpose of predator control is not to enact retribution for past attacks; it is to prevent future ones. It was at this moment, mulling over the ethical implications of her captivity and impending death, that I caught a glimpse of the mongoose's bright, terrified eyes. Remembering the explanation of how future mongooses would be attracted to the cage, I imagined her death being just the first falling domino in a series of fatal repetitions, like a grim mongoose version of the film *Groundhog Day*, and I knew that there was no way I could justify nonintervention. Doing nothing would be the catalyst of my professionally rationalized complicity in a potential chain reaction of legally sanctioned—but, at least to me, morally unjust—death.

I knelt next to the mongoose trap. A tiny growl vibrated in the mongoose's throat. I lifted the door, and she darted out, disappearing into the grass. I felt a confusing mix of triumph and shame. I had acted on what I felt was a moral duty to help the mongoose avoid an unfair death, but I also felt like I failed in my responsibilities as both a participant observer and a sanctuary volunteer. In acting outside the taken-for-granted ethics of engagement, I gained an unexpected experience in affectively participating in complex moral dilemmas that seriously impact the lives of other animal individuals. I felt firsthand the messiness of making hard choices that cannot be adequately resolved through professional objective detachment or reductive legal valuations of life.

Back at the main barn, Seth asked me if I had seen anything in the trap. "No," I lied, "the bait was gone but the trap was empty." Olivia said that it was probably not set correctly and sent Seth to redo it. My dishonesty compounded my guilt, and I began to second-guess my actions, worrying that I might be enabling more bird deaths at the jaws of a hungry mongoose.

When I arrived at the sanctuary the next morning, Seth told me that they had found a mongoose in the cage. Glumly, he explained that he shot her with a BB gun and threw her body in the tall grass along the property line. Fearing that my actions had been futile, I hoped that at least the mongoose I had freed had stayed away from the cage. The following day, one of the interns told Olivia that there was yet another mongoose in the trap. My sense of futility only intensified as I wondered how many more mongooses would be attracted to the blood around the trap. I felt grief both for the mongoose who had already died and the ones who would follow. On top of and amplifying the grief, I felt frustration that I had not been able to do more to help them.

I soon discovered I was not alone in these feelings. I heard Seth tell Olivia that he did not think he could kill mongooses anymore. She told him, "We have to; it's part of our predator control plan."

"I know," Seth said unhappily.

Olivia took the other two interns back to show them how to shoot the mongoose while Seth and I stayed in the main barn. I asked him why he did not want to shoot the new mongoose.

"I had an epiphany last night. I just don't feel right about it," he told me. I remembered how glum he seemed about shooting the mongoose the day before. "If the gun were an automatic, I'd be okay with it, but the BB gun requires reloading. It only takes a couple of seconds, but that's too long if you've already hit the mongoose with a shot that didn't kill it. That's what happened with the last one. I missed its skull the first time and had to shoot it again to kill it. They probably can't feel anything at that point, but it still doesn't feel right to me. I decided I just can't do it anymore. It's for me, so I can sleep at night."

"I understand how you feel," I said, though I did not tell him about my own encounter with the mongoose.

"It's a losing battle anyway," he added. "For every one you kill, there's twenty waiting to take its place."

As I pondered Seth's sense of futility over the act of killing a mongoose and how it mirrored my own over the act of trying to rescue one, I also had an epiphany. In seeing intervention as diametrically opposed to my professional responsibilities as an observer, I was creating a false dichotomy. Not intervening to help the mongoose would have left me feeling complicit in her death—just as Seth did now—even if I could justify my noninterference as professional conduct. I knew this to be true because, despite my rationalizations, I already felt complicit in the deaths of the mice that I had witnessed. It now seems to me that ignoring the significance of grief and its impetus to action in such circumstances may be another kind of trap, in this case imprisoning the researcher rather than the mongoose. This trap intensifies the sense of irreconcilability between the ethical responsibility to act and the professional responsibility to observe. However, treating grief and its potential impetus to action as a valid and important dimension of research encounters with death and suffering may help to bridge these two responsibilities, making intervention not only the appropriate response but also precisely what should be observed by a researcher in those moments. In this case, I understood Seth's response better because I also chose to act in response to (in my case, anticipatory) feelings about being complicit in the death of a mongoose.

Intervention may not always be possible or effective, and "appropriate" responses are often unclear and open to debate. It is certainly impossible to prevent the deaths or suffering of every gazelle or starving child or mongoose. But regardless of how one responds to it, merely experiencing grief in the field reveals the impossibility of true professional detachment. As researchers, we are already deeply entangled with the beings we study, and—at least sometimes—intervening when we can to stop or minimize death and suffering can also be a mode of observation, providing new and otherwise inaccessible insights and understandings. In this case, my grief arose from my encounter with a real embodied individual facing the violent effects of being valued less than the other lives in a reductive legal hierarchy. My subsequent intervention on her behalf enabled me to understand the mutually constitutive dynamic between grief and (in)action in such circumstances in a more nuanced, complex way than I could have if I had only observed Seth's reaction.

NOTES

1. This material is based on work supported by the National Science Foundation under grant number 1322203.

2. Maureen Ryan, "The Death of Kevin Carter and One Indelible Image," *Chicago Tribune*, August 15, 2015, http://featuresblogs.chicago tribune.com/entertainment_tv/2006/08/the_death_of_ke.html.

3. The names of informants, field sites, and individual animals have been changed to preserve anonymity.

4. Social scientists have critiqued the concept of "invasive species" to reveal how it both reinforces racist or xenophobic spatial ideologies about who or what belongs within national boundaries and contributes to hierarchies of value that render certain species killable while protecting others. See, e.g., Jean Comaroff and John L. Comaroff,

"Naturing the Nation: Aliens, Apocalypse and the Postcolonial State," *Journal of Southern African Studies* 27, no. 3 (2001): 627–51; Eben Kirksey, *Emergent Ecologies* (Durham, NC: Duke University Press, 2015); Fiona Probyn-Rapsey, "The Cultural Politics of Eradication: Dingos" (paper presented at the Human Animal Studies Seminar Series, Columbia University, New York, NY, September 27, 2016); and Thom van Dooren, "Invasive Species in Penguin Worlds: An Ethical Taxonomy of Killing for Conservation," *Conservation and Society* 9, no. 4 (2011): 286–98.

5. In the Hawaiian context, alien or nonnative species are any species that were introduced to the islands with human assistance. Hawaiian Invasive Species Council, "Invasive Species," accessed June 21, 2017, http://dlnr.hawaii.gov/hisc/info/; Hawaiian Administrative Rules §13-124-2, accessed June 21, 2017, http://dlnr.hawaii.gov/dofaw/files/2013/09/Chap124a.pdf.

6. At the time of writing, there is an active program targeting mongooses only on the island of Kauai, though in 2016, the Hawaiian Department of Land and Natural Resources and the US Fish and Wildlife Service began holding public hearings to investigate how best to expand their efforts to control mongoose and rodent populations on the islands. See Bret Yager, "State, Feds Propose Greater Mongoose, Rodent Controls," *Hawaii Tribune Herald*, February 25, 2016, http://hawaiitribune-herald.com/news/local-news/state-feds-propose-greater-mongoose-rodent-controls.

7. The relevant statute prohibits mutilating, poisoning, or killing any animal "other than insects, vermin, or other pests; provided that the handling or extermination of any insect, vermin, or other pest is conducted in accordance with standard and acceptable pest control practices and all applicable laws and regulations." Hawaiian Penal Code §711-1109(c), accessed June 21, 2017, www.capitol.hawaii.gov/hrscurrent/Vol14_Ch0701-0853/HRS0711/HRS_0711-1109.htm.

BIBLIOGRAPHY

Comaroff, Jean, and John L. Comaroff. "Naturing the Nation: Aliens, Apocalypse and the Postcolonial State." *Journal of Southern African Studies* 27, no. 1 (2001): 627–51.

Hawaiian Administrative Rules §13-124-2. Accessed June 21, 2017. http://dlnr.hawaii.gov/dofaw/files/2013/09/Chap124a.pdf.

Hawaiian Invasive Species Council. "Invasive Species." Accessed June 21, 2017. http://dlnr.hawaii.gov/hisc/info/.

Hawaiian Penal Code §711-1109(c). Accessed June 21, 2017. www.capitol. hawaii.gov/hrscur rent/Vol14_Cho701-0853/HRS0711/HRS_0711-1109.htm.

Kirksey, Eben. *Emergent Ecologies*. Durham, NC: Duke University Press, 2015.

Probyn-Rapsey, Fiona. "The Cultural Politics of Eradication: Dingos." Paper presented at the Human Animal Studies Seminar Series, Columbia University, New York, NY, September 27, 2016.

Ryan, Maureen. "The Death of Kevin Carter and One Indelible Image." *Chicago Tribune*, August 15, 2015. http://featuresblogs.chicag otribune.com/entertainment_tv/2006/08/the_death_of_ke.html.

van Dooren, Thom. "Invasive Species in Penguin Worlds: An Ethical Taxonomy of Killing for Conservation." *Conservation and Society* 9, no. 4 (2011): 286–98.

Yager, Bret. "State, Feds Propose Greater Mongoose, Rodent Controls." *Hawaii Tribune Herald*, February 25, 2016. http://hawaiitribune-herald .com/news/local-news/state-feds-propose-greater-mongoose-rode nt-controls.

CHAPTER FIVE

The Authentic Hypocrisy
of Ecological Grief

AMY SPARK

Facing east, the spring breeze cools my back from the climb up Lesueur Ridge. It is a brilliantly sunny Alberta afternoon—the kind they make postcards of. All I can hear are the dry twigs snapping under my feet and the distant hum of the occasional car on Highway 40 to the south. The smells are intoxicating: hints of spring growth and dry grass, but the smell that assails my nostrils is one of freshly cut wood. It reminds me of camp-fires, carpentry with my father, and my childhood tent trailer.

What seems out of place is the destruction stretched out before me. My sight and sense of smell are painting two disparate pictures. Acres of open slopes where trees recently stood. Stumps as tombstones, machine tracks as scars, and a few thin trees as a testament to what was once here. The clear-cut happened so recently that the smell of chainsaws and cut wood is still heavy in the air. So, this is what it feels like to miss the forest for the trees.

Except . . . what am I feeling? Despair? Shock? The emotional jolt I had been warned about by my interview participants? No. In fact . . . almost nothing really. It isn't even numbness. All I can think about is how good it smells, how invigorated I am from the hike, and how guilty I feel for not experiencing remorse, sadness, or ecological grief—the focus of my research and the reason for my climb.

. . .

The pages of this volume are filled with ethical considerations and complexities surrounding experiences of grief. However, I suggest that at the societal level, grief is generally seen as a straightforward, normalized reaction to the loss of something precious and dear. Most commonly discussed is the grief followed by the death of a loved one. But research has shown that one may also grieve the death of a beloved job, pet, or home.[1] These are forms of disenfranchised death: those that are "seldom acknowledged, publicly mourned, or socially supported."[2] While studying environmental degradation in the Ghost River Valley in Alberta, Canada, I stumbled on another form of disenfranchised loss: the death of an ecosystem.

Canada has been identified as a particularly death-adverse society: one that is "death denying" and that bureaucratizes grief.[3] This manifests as recommended bereavement leave durations, expensive and formalized funeral proceedings, and societal expectations around the length and format of grieving. Reactions and discussions surrounding death are often subdued or entirely avoided. Nevertheless, when the word *grief* is used (as it seldom is during "polite conversation"), it conjures loss and sadness rather than bureaucracy. The term incites empathy in those hearing of a loss, and it levels the playing field. Although people may not grieve in the same way or for the same length of time, almost everyone grieves at some point in their life. It is an equal-opportunity emotion.

As a Canadian scholar-activist, I strive to disrupt our societal aversion to discussing loss. I seek to legitimize the term and experience of *ecological grief* within the context of Alberta. So, as the term *ecological grief* becomes used and normalized, it begins to conjure and communicate the depth of the emotions that are felt after a perceived loss in the environment. As with other forms of grief, my hope is that it acts as an equalizer and entry point into empathy between groups and individuals. While on this journey, however, I personally wrestle with the entanglements of grief, guilt, and hypocrisy. How do grief and guilt manifest in the face of environmental change, particularly when fellow humans and one's own community are the perpetrators of the crime, and we are all enjoying the economic benefits to some degree? It is in this state of personal turmoil that I have written this piece.

•   •   •

Later that same day, I find myself amid the quietness of a forested ecosystem. The air is much cooler now; I can feel the temperature dropping as the sun sets behind me. There is still enough light to see pink streaks across the skyline, a skunk ambling ahead, and the wetland to my right. My boots are still dusty from the hike earlier. I'm walking with a resident of the area, hearing his story about the upcoming clear-cut. He's speaking very pragmatically: in six months, this area will look like the area I saw this morning. In fact, it's already being called Cutblock 3049 by both the residents and the logging company. My companion and I may be some of the last people to walk in this section of forest. We wait for the skunk to pass, then continue, chatting about hydrology and birch trees as we go.

We come to a stand of trees, some marked with pink surveyors' ribbons. The ribbons denote a future logging road and mark the trees for the guillotine. Now, a road hovering in midair materializes in my mind. I wonder about our skunk companion from earlier and where they will find refuge once the trees are gone. As we continue to chat, our pauses lengthen. The

air seems slightly heavier, the lightness and pragmatism of our earlier con-
versation gone. And there it is—that tightness in my stomach that I was
expecting—six hours too late. A small burning in the back of my throat as
I think about the totality of what will be lost: trees, skunks, wetlands,
grasses, fungi, birds, mosses, the sound of wind in the trees, habitats, rela-
tionships, and solace. I realize that I had to see what previously existed,
before I could truly feel or understand what it means for the place to be
changed. Earlier, I was looking at a landscape that hinted at a memory of
a forest. But that memory wasn't complete; it missed the poetry of this place.

. . .

I think a lot about my guilt from that earlier hike. Guilt for *not*
feeling other emotions such as sadness. It made me question not
only my own identity as a naturalist but also whether my
research participants were exaggerating their experiences. Or, I
wondered if my interpretation of their experiences was skewed.
This doubt added to my guilt—here I was, attempting not only
to bring their stories to light but also to examine them deeply,
all the while balancing my distance as a researcher with my
sympathy. If everyone felt such deep sadness and hopelessness
when viewing a clear-cut site, where was my compassion? My
grief?

I was the unfeeling soul who laughs at a funeral.

Yet, to laugh at a funeral—especially with others—can be a
helpful way to mourn. It provides a relief, a brief respite from
the heaviness of the day. I imagine now my time up on Lesueur
Ridge not as inappropriate detachment but as a break from the
heaviness of interviewing and a joy at using my muscles. My
grief came later, after I had time to process what a clear-cut site
meant and the completeness of the loss. I realized my guilt about
my delayed emotional reaction wasn't the whole story. Rather, it

was just one step in the story of my own ecological grief. My guilt became entangled with my fears about my inaugural research project and my simultaneous labels of *objective researcher* and *impassioned naturalist*. Over time I have begun to realize that my guilt is part of the larger experience of my own despair over environmental changes.

Guilt is just as important to this story as grief. Although I have been able to unpack my guilt, I was not alone in experiencing self-blame and resentment. This was an emotion embedded in almost every interview I did with residents, activists, and proprietors in the area. However, this guilt and self-appointed blame had less to do with the expectancy of certain emotions, and more to do with the sociopolitical region in which the logging was taking place.

Alberta is a province with a conservative political and religious history and an economy based almost exclusively on resource extraction: primarily oil and gas, with forestry and mining as siblings. It is a province that grapples with a history of systemic oppression of Indigenous groups—oppression that still echoes today despite reconciliation efforts. It is an area that values hard work, innovation, and a strong conservation ethic. An area where the largest city is within a forty-five-minute drive of wilderness and home to the first national park in Canada. A region that experienced a destructive flood in 2013 and disastrous fire in 2016, yet prides itself on being resilient. An area where environmental groups are funded primarily by energy companies. A region with one of the highest per capita carbon footprints in the *world*, due to lifestyle and geography.[4] A place that, in 2015, swung the pendulum politically, voting in a progressive government after forty years of conservative leadership. This is the system that breeds complicated emotions like guilt and abstract blame, and where conservation and resource-extraction ethics come into conflict.

Those residents I spoke with named three versions of their guilt as it related to their condemnation of the ongoing clear-cut logging practices in the area. First, they identified their guilt over the use of wood products in their own lives. How can you grieve a forest when you also live in a house made of timber? Second, many are working in a resource-extraction sector themselves, predominantly the petroleum industry. How dare you grieve the loss of forest through logging when you contribute, either directly or indirectly, to the loss and destruction of landscapes each day? Last, esoteric guilt about living in a capitalist society that condones clear-cut forestry and other detrimental land-use practices. How can you grieve something when you were part of a complacent society that enabled this loss to happen and continues to enable this destruction? These were the types of questions people were asking themselves and internalizing. Although these sentiments were evident in interviews, these are not usually the types of questions discussed among Albertans in their daily lives. How many others are silently grappling with these questions every day?

When one lives in a province that is heavily dependent on resource extraction nestled within a country where grief is bureaucratized, the mere expression of ecological grief is interpreted as a political statement. To grieve a portion of the landscape is to pass judgment on the political parties, organizations, communities, and individuals who are perceived to have caused the destruction. To grieve is also to make an abstract statement about one's role in the system. One may work in a resource-extraction sector or have close family and friends who do; one may work for a conservation advocacy organization financially supported by the petroleum sector. Even if it is possible to remove oneself from these ties, by using the spatially diffuse and automobile-centric infrastructure found in Alberta, one is contributing to the highest carbon footprint in the world.

What results from this heightened sensitivity is a culture in which expressing remorse for environmental loss or destruction seems hypocritical. In response, grief turns into guilt, guilt into shame, and shame into uncomfortable silence. No one wants to bite the hand that feeds them, nor do they want their ethics exposed for scrutiny by others. It is much safer to remain quiet.

As an Albertan, I am not disputing that we engage in highly hypocritical actions. It is a truth that I wrestle with daily. Even our current provincial government, having recently implemented a carbon tax, is actively advocating for more pipelines. However, now begins the delicate balance of *understanding* the mechanics behind the hypocritical system without *excusing* the actions within the system. This parallels my simultaneous roles within and outside the system: a human geographer studying the context in which I live. Where does my firsthand experience of living in Alberta fit into my detached, scientifically based conclusions? Where do my anger and embarrassment with the petroleum industry end, and my empathy for those working within the sector begin? I have come to realize these are not the right questions to be asking. Instead, how can my own hypocritical actions and guilt *as an Albertan* be used as an asset and leverage for communication?

When grief is labeled as merely a hypocritical action (as in Ghost Valley), the richness of the story behind those mixed emotions and the potential to use the experience toward change are overlooked. My lack of "proper" emotions when observing a clear-cut could have been the end of the story. Instead, I discovered that my premature guilt was unfounded—I *did* feel ecological grief, but differently than was expected or explained to me. I felt it only after I experienced the fullness of the ecosystem. I wonder what stories, lessons, and truths have yet to be uncovered by the complicated emotions felt by the Ghost Valley community.

Instead of hypocrisy as the *end* to a conversation—the final blow to one's credibility—I believe it's where the conversation should begin. The discourse can evolve past "One does not have the *right* to grieve because of one's role in the system" to "*Why* does one continue to grieve natural spaces if they believe they are part of the system that has contributed to the destruction?" or "What outcomes does this grief have if it continues to go unnamed and not legitimized?" Perhaps most hopefully we can ask: What *could* happen if one had the social sanction to voice their environmental distress? Could the emotional lens be integrated into environmental assessments? Could we begin to see ourselves as emotional, loving beings capable of change rather than merely hypocrites?

I have asserted that to grieve ecologically is perceived as a political act or statement in Alberta. Yet I see my work as promoting the transfer of ecological grief from the political realm to the apolitical. For it is not the grief itself that is political, but the guilt that follows—the *expression* of this grief within the sociopolitical climate and capitalist society of Alberta. The grief doesn't become hypocritical until it is externalized and correlated to political ideology, employment choice, and identity. Scholarship about ecological grief should take social and political context into account, certainly. But my interest as a scholar-activist is in how ecological grief influences individual and community health, and how it can be used as transformative language for positive change.

By labeling ecological grief as merely "political," we obscure the spiritual, personal, familial, and physical ties to the landscape. To grieve ecologically says more (or should say more) about one's relationship to place than it does about their job title, political stance, or place of residence. What I found through my research and personal experience is that ecological grief is more about place attachment, mental health, and memory than it is about resource extraction.

.   .   .

I sit on a small log gazing west, not a clear-cut in sight. I'm farther south in the Rocky Mountains, a year after my interviews and engagement with the Ghost Valley. My hiking boots are once again on my feet, but this time they're dusted with snow rather than soil. I breathe in deeply, searching for a scent I can ground myself in. But with the snow on the ground, the smells are dampened. Instead, I notice my heightened sense of hearing—it is silent. Gloriously silent.

What begins to creep in, as always, is that voice in the back of my head: enjoy this natural beauty while it lasts, while there's still snow in the spring, while there is silence in the mountains, and while I have the health to bring me here. I sit with these emotions for a time: this anticipatory grief, this restlessness, this powerlessness, this faint anger. Grief for this quiet place, restlessness to get the work done, powerlessness for not knowing where to begin, and anger at my own role in the system.

Sometime later, I slowly recognize I'm no longer thinking of loss. I'm thinking of the beauty again.

.   .   .

I have begun to see hypocrisy and environmental guilt as a meaningful and authentic tool for engagement. Recognizing and acknowledging grief and guilt can be an effective way to move contentious and political conversations forward. This is a small social experiment on my part—injecting the term *ecological grief* into conversation over dinner parties and work lunches. Reflecting on all that I learned from my research, I ponder what this language could do for Albertans. Using the word *grief*—a term that already exists to describe a fundamentally human experience— incites empathy. It allows us to move beyond the surface-level guilt that we may feel by living hypocritically. Through use of this common language, we can begin discussing the issue people are grappling with: that changes to landscape can have deep effects on our mental and emotional health. That loss can evoke a range of (sometimes contradictory) emotions. That these complications are something we should be talking about. And in an area where *forest* means *sanctuary* to some and *merchantable wood* to others, creating a common language is a transformative place to begin.

NOTES

1. On the grief experienced with the loss of a job, see William A. Borgen and Norman E. Amundson, "The Dynamics of Unemployment," *Journal of Counseling and Development* 66, no. 4 (1987): 180–84; on the loss of pets, see Marc A. Rosenberg, *Companion Animal Loss and Pet Owner Grief* (Allentown, PA: ALPO Pet Center, 1986); on the loss of a home, see Colin M. Parkes, *Bereavement* (New York: International Universities Press, 1974).

2. Herbert Northcott and Donna Wilson, *Dying and Death in Canada*, 2nd ed. (Buffalo, NY: Broadview Press, 2008), 107.

3. Philippe Ariès, *Western Attitudes toward Death: From the Middle Ages to the Present* (Baltimore: John Hopkins University Press, 1974); Northcott and Wilson, *Dying and Death in Canada*, 107.

4. Environment and Climate Change Canada, "Greenhouse Gas Emissions by Province and Territory," accessed March 27, 2017, www .ec.gc.ca/indicateurs-indicators/default.asp?lang=en&n=18F3BB9C-1.

BIBLIOGRAPHY

Ariès, Philippe. *Western Attitudes toward Death: From the Middle Ages to the Present.* Baltimore: John Hopkins University Press, 1974.

Borgen, William A., and Norman E. Amundson. "The Dynamics of Unemployment." *Journal of Counseling and Development* 66, no. 4 (1987): 180–84.

Environment and Climate Change Canada. "Greenhouse Gas Emissions by Province and Territory." Accessed March 27, 017. www.ec.gc.ca/indicateurs-indicators/default.asp?lang=en&n=18F3BB9C-1.

Northcott, Herbert, and Donna Wilson. *Dying and Death in Canada.* 2nd ed. Buffalo, NY: Broadview Press, 2008.

Parkes, Colin M. *Bereavement.* New York: International Universities Press, 1974.

Rosenberg, Marc A. *Companion Animal Loss and Pet Owner Grief.* Allentown, PA: ALPO Pet Center, 1986.

CHAPTER SIX

Scale-Blocking Grief

Witnessing the Intimate between a Conflict
Leopard and Confinement

KALLI F. DOUBLEDAY

I quietly asked the guard standing close to the caged leopardess, "What is the end?" He knew what my clumsy question meant. "It's better than to be dead," he replied. I stood face-to-face with a "conflict" leopard living out whatever life she had left in a six-by-five-foot cage. This is not an unusual occurrence in human-wildlife conflict-prone India.[1] The human communities living in and near the jungles in Rajasthan and Maharashtra, India, experience high rates of human-leopard conflict.[2] At one point, the Forest Department housed seven conflict leopards in the makeshift animal detention center where I stood (see Figure 6.1). The leopardess I locked eyes with had been a former captive, attacking and killing six people after she was released from her first detention. Even then, the priority was to tranquilize and confine; killing was the last resort.

I study human-carnivore interactions in Rajasthan and Maharashtra, an area of research concerned with the loss of both human and animal life. Over two years, in both Indian

Figure 6.1. A makeshift holding area for conflict leopards.

states, I had special permission to accompany forest officials and wildlife rescuers for weeks at a time. Both groups are perpetually involved in conflict mitigation and interview people who have experienced recent and often tragic encounters with leopards and tigers.

Grief over the loss of human life following conflict with leopards and tigers, as well as fear of future attacks, motivate practices of capturing and confining large cats in these regions. Thus, the conditions that led to the confinement of this leopardess are produced by grief; at the same time, grief permeated my own research process: not only in hearing stories in interviews with bereaved families but also in my ongoing grief over the punishment of animals who have killed humans. These layers of grief were compounded when I witnessed the captive leopardess's anguish. In this chapter, I focus on the overwhelming grief I felt during our brief encounter. What follows is an effort to unpack the reality that despite how grief is supposed to function in conservation-focused fieldwork, it permeates across multiple scales.

Figure 6.2. The leopardess in her third year of confinement and her reaction to the author.

Eye to eye, I peered into the cage lifted off the ground. This was the same cage used to capture her three years ago. True to their name, trap cages are short-term mobility devices that are not meant to confine a living animal permanently. Her distinctive smell came wafting toward me. It was pungent, like heavy dandruff from a Labrador retriever mixed with salty sweat. She looked sick with boredom. However, when I stepped closer, she violently recoiled at my proximity. Then, she pushed her crinkled forehead right up to the bars, as close to me as she could get. Her muscles contracted. Her thin whiskers jerked up and down; baring her teeth, she hissed and thundered at me (see Figure 6.2). She was a killer of humans, of me without this barrier.

I realized it likely wasn't anger or rage I was witnessing in her reaction, but fear. My stillness finally reassured her I was not a threat, and her flexed muscles relaxed back into her skin. She surrendered to her placement and lack of effective intimidation to make me flee. I blended into the unnatural surroundings she had become dulled to after three years of confinement. Her eyes stared absently into the green tarp that encircled her cage, visually separating her from the surrounding jungle. Just on the other side of the sheet of green plastic was her former territory. She had not moved far, physically. The sounds of other big cats, the smell of bear scat, and noisy foraging of wild animals at night near the cage made the plastic separation obsolete in many ways. She was still in the jungle and partially, physically, and sensorily in her place, but without the ability to live in it. Witnessing the nature of her punishment—a lifetime of confinement in a tiny cage, so close to what were once the expansive natural surroundings in which she had roamed and hunted—broke something in me.

As we turned and walked away, I heard another visitor say, "At least they did not kill her." To the Forest Department, her captive life is a successful check mark of detaining a conflict leopard, preferable to another tally under the "killed" column. Reading documents that trace the fates of conflict leopards in the "detained" or "killed" columns is one thing; for me, seeing the inhumane conditions under which some interned leopards live is another entirely. Something shifted in me at that moment, and I could no longer subscribe to the notion that a life in extreme confinement is better than death, the lesser of two evils, to justify grievous welfare. This resistance on my part is a result of witnessing the leopardess's embodied conditions in full color (and the nonhuman consequences of conflict animal detainment), almost as a participant complicit in her confinement, as a guest of the forest guards.

This leopard is not the only wild animal I have emotionally connected with. I have assisted in relocating more than a hundred wild animals from hostile situations (e.g., trapped in homes, businesses, and farms) across Rajasthan. But not all attempted rescues are successful. When the rescue team is too late, the animal may be killed, or officials may declare the animal too dangerous for release and cart them off for life in captivity. In this case, I haplessly anguish over the animal's unknown future. It is not just the loss of life, freedom, or mobility for that individual that saddens me. My mind cannot help but "scale up." I am almost immediately overtaken by thoughts of the realities of wildlife everywhere—losing habitat, without their ability to travel and behave in their "natural" ways, losing their lives to the extent of entire species' endangerment. Or, moreover, that most species have already been locally extinct from dozens if not hundreds of locations. When faced with the suffering of an individual animal, this broader, global context of the population (the species) is what I grieve. This stems from my adoption of the conservation biology mentality of "a discipline with a deadline" in the sense that time is running out to reverse trends of species endangerment and extinction.[3] Most critical, time is running out to maintain a world with large predators. With this mentality, worry for individuals or fighting battles over single animals is futile. I am accustomed to pushing the individual aside to focus on the bigger picture—the survival of the species. I call this maneuver *scale-blocking*: blocking the intimate, individual scale (and its emotional implications) and replacing it with a focus on the larger-scale implications and connections.

Based on my past experiences and my area of study, I should have scale-blocked the intimate when I encountered the leopardess in her cage. The encounter should have triggered the scaling up that reveals the broader, global implications of her singular captivity. Indeed, she reflects many significant regional and global trends. Her capture and confinement are the outcome of widespread habitat loss, increased human population and development initiatives, and the overall degradation of India's most wild places. More specifically, this leopardess's condition is the materialization of several major contextual facts in India: protected areas are predominantly conserved and designated for tigers; leopards avoid high-density tiger areas and are highly adaptable—wedging themselves between core forest areas occupied by tigers and rural village and agricultural lands. In these liminal spaces, they can come into conflict with people. As a result of these frequent encounters, the number of captured conflict leopards far outweighs the amount of open zoo space to confine them. The lack of resources for forest department officials means that leopard housing is usually unsatisfactory in space and quality. The intersection of these many conservation issues at the species level resembles my typical emotional pattern when confronted with a singular, suffering wild life. However, something different—unsettling—happened when I encountered the caged leopardess. I grieved for *this leopardess.* And grieving her, individually, without the subsequent intimate scale-blocking, felt highly unusual for me as a scientist. Her distinctive rage, defeat, and fear framed by a literal cage of persecution and power dynamics culminate in grief just for *her,* the individual. I am unable to push her embodied experience away and scale up.

Our encounter resulted in an unshakable rewiring in how I think and feel about my research. It is no longer so easy for me to scale up or abstract from the individual, but something else, more profound and unsettling, has also happened. I can now not think of the abstracted work of conservation without thinking about *this leopardess.* The terms *conflict animal, human-wildlife con-*

flict, and *leopard* instantly replay *her* struggle, stress, communication, and physical restraint in my mind. Now, my memory of her is where my thoughts go when I think of, hear, or read those words. When this happens, I worry over a set of questions that get at the heart of this shift I have experienced in my identity as a researcher, conservationist, and emotional being: Am I allowed to grieve an individual animal? Am I permitted to give one individual this mental and emotional space when my wider intellectual exploration concerns species that span taxonomic and geographic boundaries? Shouldn't her story and my witnessing it merely emphasize the larger scale issues at play in this tragedy? It used to.

These questions are especially meaningful to me as I continue to volunteer as a wildlife rescuer in India. I struggled in the agonizing moments I spent witnessing this one specific leopardess to block the scale of the individual and scale up to the population. I struggled to engage in the abstraction so central to a conservation scientist's ethic. I struggled to move my mind and heart away from her, away from her agony, away from witnessing her grief. I especially did not expect this new lightning-fast mental connection between her-the-individual, and the wider literature, research, and projects that are not about her, the individual. Yet, years later, my memory of her is immediately triggered when I engage in this work. And I have to ask: What role does grief for the singular animal play in conservation work? Could an attention to grief—to all emotions felt in the moment of encounter—transform how conservationists, researchers, and people who encounter free-living and captive animals think about and practice their work?

This attention to the emotional and the centering of the singular animal has been productive in my thought process. As an academic researcher, it crystallized the reality that the study of human-carnivore conflict and/or interactions is not only about negotiating shared space and the territoriality of animals and humans overlapping in a way that results in conflict. It is also about the suffering endured by individual people and animals involving the painful restriction of space and the experience of being displaced. This leopardess brought me to the edge of many questions repeated and theorized across disciplines: What is an animal life worth living? In line with Judith Butler's work, what makes a life grievable, but moreover, a nonhuman life grievable to a researcher?[4] By conceding to my inner debate on the politics of the individual and seeing her, the leopardess, my rewired mental connections anchor me, to see down to the intimate to better look back up and see the connections from below instead of above.

As she likely continues to languish there, I write down her story while simultaneously asking: Is it important enough for me to take up this much space for her story and not just my processing of it? As storytellers, can qualitative researchers tell individual animal stories in productive ways? Do we have to analyze what we cannot evaluate to its truest meaning, her communication from her confinement? Can I simply tell her story, and in that be a (her) political agent? Many scholars from diverse fields are taking on the effort to tell individual animal stories through multispecies ethnography.[5] In a different form, my experience with this leopardess solidified new research questions around the individual. People's grief over the deteriorating health of the tigress named Machli became the focal point of research to explore the liminality of a "famous" wild life woven in and out of the in situ and ex situ conservation landscape.[6] This research did not include Machli's voice itself but is evidence of the need to tell individual animals' stories. Likewise, the leopardess's story told here was narrated at a national conference, in an article, and is now part of this edited volume's broader narrative. The individual Other in conservation landscapes is an important and emerging field of inquiry that I now participate in as a consequence of my dwelling at the intimate scale.

The leopardess's grief inevitably manifests in other confined conflict animals witnessed by the forests guards who are assigned to keep them caged. The grief that moved from the leopardess to me also takes form in the guards as sadness and guilt. The movement of emotion across species enduring and witnessing grief is evident here among several human stakeholders. Two guards I spoke with, who have been part of the network keeping this suffering in place, described years of their own suffering that overshadowed but echoed mine after my single encounter.

However, there were also guards who did not reveal any form of discomfort or long-term anguish over the non-zoo-placed (excess) conflict animals' conditions. This caused me concern, knowing I was being witnessed by some who were not able (or willing) to empathize with the leopardess or my palpable reaction. Gatekeepers of my research goals were noting my reaction. Would my blatant disapproval or (at minimum) unease at official Forest Department protocol block my research progress and career goals as a result? How could I be bothered with such thoughts? There they were, ephemeral and momentary thoughts dimming my concern for the nonhuman individual by centering my own needs and desires.

I only encountered her that one time, but I entered into her agony, if only minimally, through her cross-species communication that penetrated the barrier providing fluid access to empathize. This personal transformation is now a constant reminder not only that there is *room* for grieving the ungrievable, the individual nonhuman, but that it is a *necessity*. To avoid grief in the field, we allow ourselves to scale up, blurring or retreating from the pain of confronting the suffering before us. In so doing, we blur the ethical issue before our eyes by filling our perspective with the larger issues our research engages. We zoom out to unacceptable rates of global biodiversity and habitat loss in looking past singular injustices. This is one step in the devaluing of nonhuman and human life that guides most personal and state laws across the world. This can happen when we perpetually scale up as a way to scale-block the intimate. It is framed as the professional choice: detachment and continual generalizations. It is framed as the choice of personal preservation: limiting our emotional labor to maintain a productive trajectory. It is also framed as the apolitical choice: to be unbiased, only an observer, not a pallbearer, not a griever. Antithetically, I have found, for me, the individual—the leopard, *this* leopardess—anchors all the rest.

NOTES

1. A conflict leopard is deemed removable from the wild by government officials based on their ongoing threat to people and/or livestock.

2. Laurie Marker and Swarnatara Sivamani, "Policy for Human-Leopard Conflict Management in India," *CAT News*, no. 50 (2009): 23–26; Sachin Saini, "Leopard Attacks Spur Action Plan, Focus on Prey Base," *Hindustan Times*, February 11, 2017.

3. "Discipline with a deadline" is attributed to Edward O. Wilson, "Biodiversity: Vanishing before Our Eyes," *Time* 155, no. 16A (Special Earth Day Edition, April/May 2000): 28–34.

4. On grievability, see Judith Butler, *Frames of War: When Is Life Grievable?* (London: Verso, 2009).

5. Kathryn Gillespie, *The Cow with Ear Tag #1389* (Chicago: University of Chicago Press, 2018); Marcus Baynes-Rock, "Shared Responsibility in a Multispecies Playground," *Between the Species* 17, no. 1 (2013): 6, http://digitalcommons.calpoly.edu/bts/vol17/iss1/6.

6. Kalli F. Doubleday, "Nonlinear Liminality: Human-Animal Relations on Preserving the World's Most Famous Tigress." *Geoforum* no. 81 (2017): 32–44.

BIBLIOGRAPHY

Baynes-Rock, Marcus. "Shared Responsibility in a Multispecies Playground." *Between the Species* 17, no. 1 (2013): Art. 6, http://digitalcommons.calpoly.edu/bts/vol17/iss1/6.

Butler, Judith. *Frames of War: When Is Life Grievable?* London: Verso, 2009.

Doubleday, Kalli F. "Nonlinear Liminality: Human-Animal Relations on Preserving the World's Most Famous Tigress." *Geoforum* 81 (May 2017): 32–44.

Gillespie, Kathryn. *The Cow with Ear Tag #1389*. Chicago: University of Chicago Press, 2018.

Marker, Laurie, and Swarnatara Sivamani. "Policy for Human-Leopard Conflict Management in India." *CAT News* 50 (2009): 23–26.

Saini, Sachin. "Leopard Attacks Spur Action Plan, Focus on Prey Base." *Hindustan Times*, February 11, 2017.

Wilson, Edward O. "Biodiversity: Vanishing before Our Eyes," *Time* 155, no. 16A (Special Earth Day Edition, April/May 2000): 28–34.

CHAPTER SEVEN

On Missing People in the Field

DAVID BOARDER GILES

I don't know what happened to M. I don't think anybody does—except, I hope, M. himself.

Just when things seemed to be looking up, he left. When he finally had a roof over his head, when I had discovered how to reach his family in Iran, he packed up his room at the shelter and told his caseworker he was leaving for the airport to go home.

But I'd never had a chance to give him their number. He never said good-bye. It's not impossible that he found another way to contact them. Or that a kind soul bought him a ticket. Or that, by some miracle, the Transportation Security Agency let him—a bearded, unkempt, paranoid Middle Easterner with broken English—onto the plane and he made the journey without incident.

But it seems unlikely. I imagine the worst. (My hands shake as I type out, then delete my speculations.)

There's a chance I'll run into him out of the blue, maybe the next time I'm in Seattle. Perhaps we'll have the same old conversation. He'll ask if I've finished my studies and tell me to go back home to Australia. He'll tell me that the bank stole his money. That the police harassed him. *This country is no good*, he'll say.

But there's no comfort in the uncertainty. It's as opaque and unsettling as the rest of our friendship. In seven years, I had struggled to piece together anything beyond this plausible but fragmented refrain. I met him at the beginning of my doctoral research. I was writing about homelessness and the politics of global cities like Seattle—trying to understand precisely the political-economic forces that shape lives like his. And yet, by the time I finished, I knew barely more about him. His departure was a mystery because he was.

In many ways, he was already missing.

Yet I learned a great deal from him. He was never formally part of my fieldwork. But where ethnographic research entangles us in the lives and concerns of others, there can be no sharp distinction between research and care, and perhaps also grief. Grief, after all, is the opposite of closure. And M. haunts my work with all the urgency and openness of a question mark, one that punctuates everything I write. How does one disappear in this society of constant surveillance? Question mark. How might one get lost in the city's patchwork labyrinth of services designed to support (or warehouse) the homeless body? Question mark. How can one hide in plain sight on the public sidewalk? What else could we have done? Question mark, question mark. M. taught me concrete lessons about these urban landscapes—I'll recount them here. But above all he taught me that, for all the research I might do, there are questions I will not answer. It helps to theorize, but only a little. Mainly, I would just like to tell the story. To ask the questions. In a way, this is a missing persons report.

. . .

For most of our friendship, M.'s conversation was inscrutable. His English was as functional as the playing of a pianist who had spent a lifetime practicing "Chopsticks": equal parts fluent and fragmentary. His repertoire consisted of a single conversation about the bank and the police who harassed him and stole his money. (The order varied.) Bitterly, he would repeat the story. It wasn't clear if he had forgotten telling it already—sometimes moments before—or if he just needed to get it off his chest again. It wasn't clear whether it was a delusion or a memory. Both seemed possible.

We ran into each other unpredictably on "The Ave," University Way, where I lived and held office hours.[1] I would buy him lunch and try, in vain, to learn more. Maybe he lacked the vocabulary to add any detail to the story. Or the attention span. Or the interest. But he was grimly, singularly consistent. Like Samuel Beckett's Vladimir and Estragon, we began from first principles each time, with no hint of whether he remembered our previous conversations.[2] Except that he remembered who I was: without fail he would tell me to go home to my country. *This country is no good. These fucking police. The bank. They took my money.*

In a way, M. is for me a fiction, made of guesses and untold stories. It doesn't even feel right to give him a pseudonym.

. . .

And yet he was a friend. Six years passed as I've described, and then, after a long hiatus, I ran into him in front of one of my favorite bars on The Ave. (I did some of my best writing there; late-night regulars wandered in and filtered onto the page.) For the first time, M.'s singular demeanor softened: he seemed glad to see me. He also seemed dazed, subdued, maybe on antipsychotic drugs. He had a place to stay, he told me. Stable accommodation was a blessing, but that aside, even telling me was an achievement. We hadn't had more than one looped five-minute conversation in the preceding years. But now he seemed able to carry on longer discussions. And with some lexical fumbling, as if the endeavor were brand new, he asked me whether I had a television. No, whether I *watched* television. No, whether I *wanted* to watch television.

It dawned slowly on me that he was asking me if we could *hang out*. So I gave him my number. And later, he called me from the shelter and arranged to visit. He even asked to stay over, which he'd never done when he was shelterless. I only let him stay once, wary of how incompletely I still knew him—and also of contracting body lice, which he shed across my white sofa like cracked pepper the second time he visited. But as the weeks went on, he began using the word *friend*.

But how does one befriend an enigma?

Ours was a singular fellowship. I can't speak for him. But in the absence of common interests, shared experiences, or any appreciable surety of having the same conversation, it seemed to be based on nothing more than the bare recognition of another capable of caring and being cared for.

This is not the friendship of the familiar or the like—of kin, in-groups, populisms, like minds, or soul mates. Not the shared identity that binds us to conformity and conflict alike. Those affinities obscure the otherness that makes the very endeavor of care possible. The philosopher Martin Buber called this otherness, simply, "thou."[3] The opacity and intimacy of difference itself, without which any relationship amounts to narcissism. (If we're honest, we never wholly know the people we care about.)

The most important thing about this radical otherness isn't that we overcome it. Quite the opposite. It persists. It is the unanswered question that draws us into relationships of becoming. In this precise sense, there can be no research without care, and no care without research (although the best of us lose sight of this sometimes). This is why many of us venture into ethnographic fieldwork. Not to answer great questions, nor to capture and caricature the world at large, but out of a concern and a commitment to difference itself. We value interlocutors as yet undefined. We already care.

·   ·   ·

With our breakthroughs in the art of conversation, I was able to learn new details. But as fieldworkers and social workers alike know, answers raise new questions. M. had come to the University of Washington to study engineering. He was now in his late forties, I guessed. Had he been here for two decades? He had been back to see his family only once. When had they lost touch, and why? Had he haunted The Ave ever since?

I can only imagine what futures seemed possible for the young M. An academic migrant in the global knowledge economy, he was among the demographic for whom the new world-class Seattle would be built: information technology now drives the city's superlative growth; out-of-state tuition underwrites the university's expansion; and both of them buoy up the aspirations of real estate speculators. Cranes and gleaming apartment complexes coax well-funded international students to the once-shabby, bohemian University District.

But there is no place for him there now. The man I know couldn't remember what day or time it was, let alone attend classes. His fingernails grew too long and curled for him to use a keyboard. But homelessness is not simply a characteristic of individuals. It is a systemic process of place-making and unmaking, of constructing homes for some, and not for others (as anyone knows who has endured the crescendo of Seattle's housing costs). There were fewer and fewer places along The Ave where M.'s disposition was not likely to get him "eighty-sixed," as the bartenders and baristas called it—banished for the comfort of a more urbane, less urban clientele.

M. and the neighborhood had coevolved. As Samuel Delaney writes so movingly of Times Square's redevelopment, gentrification itself produces estrangement and vulnerability, decimating the vectors for contact across class, race, and other difference.[4] Lives like M.'s become, in Judith Butler's terms, ungrievable, failing to register as lives that matter in the public eye.[5] And so, there is scant political or economic will to make space for the relations of care and otherness that made M. and me friends. By the time I met him, he had none of the relationships that make a place home. He only occasionally talked about another "friend," the owner of an Iranian restaurant who fed him and let him sleep on the back steps sometimes. He had become, for most passersby, what Samira Kawash called "the homeless body"—the ineffable, ungrievable form coded with threat and deviance, and yet somehow also invisible, hiding in plain sight.[6]

By the time I met him, M. had already disappeared multiple times: erratic and dissociative, he fell out of touch with family; obviously homeless, he faded from view as people averted their eyes; an immigrant—probably undocumented by now—he was excluded from the entitlements of the US public. At long last, when friends or institutions did try to help, he was too far beyond our scope. I believe—I hope—we did what was within our power to help. But too little was within our power. He fell through the cracks, through our fingers, and then he was gone.

It was his caseworker who told me he'd left. We had spoken occasionally by phone, with M.'s consent. He was always warm, but brief, probably overworked and with little scope to involve me. We never met. Apparently M. simply told him he was going back to Iran, and cleared out what few belongings he had.

His caseworker gave no indication of entertaining the anxieties that I now entertained. How had M. bought a ticket? Could he have updated his passport? Could he have even boarded a plane, let alone completed the journey? He was ill-tempered and fidgety. Middle Eastern travelers have been detained for much less. And if he made it, what then? But his caseworker was matter-of-fact: M. had voluntarily checked out; there was nothing more to be done. It was beyond his purview, or that of the rest of Seattle's spotty safety net.

For years, I hadn't a clue where to turn for help. I discovered early on how naive it was to simply recommend shelters and food banks. "Shelters are good places to get stabbed, to get your stuff stolen, or to get tuberculosis," another homeless friend had told me patiently, as I sheepishly pocketed the list I had copied down for him. I later learned about Sound Mental Health from a homeless friend who heard voices. But it was a medical institution; its bureaucracy and her own disorder kept her away. I can't imagine making an intake appointment for M.

Finally, somebody offered him accommodation at a Housing First facility that operated under the principle that it is cheaper and more just to bypass housing vouchers, waiting lists, sobriety, treatment, and job interviews and instead simply house people. It sounds good, although I've heard homeless advocates jokingly refer to it as "Housing Last," since it is reserved for the chronically homeless—for whom, by definition, all else has failed. Once there, M. had counseling, medication, and the prospect of longer-term housing. The shelter even arranged field trips to the cinema. But after years of untreated mental illness, trauma, perhaps abuse (the bank, these fucking police), and alienation (this country is no good), it is an understatement to say that it was too little, and too late.

In the absence of the right help, such safety nets are at best a Band-Aid, at worst a warehouse for the poor. Indeed, Craig Willse describes them as a homeless management industry, one complicit in the policy and place-making that produces homelessness itself.[7] M.'s experience illustrates how this is possible.

· · ·

For six years, M. had said nothing about his inner life. What sort of inner monologue had he had? Was it as singular as our conversations? What interlocutors accompanied him, as he shuffled along The Ave, talking to almost nobody?

But that had changed. He seemed to be experimenting. Maybe shelter, or counseling, or medication helped, but a wall had fallen, perhaps between us, perhaps within himself. I was no better equipped to respond than his social worker.

He aired new discontents. Just when there were more people in his life than there had been in years, he said he was lonely. Maybe caseworkers and shelter guests weren't very satisfying company. Or perhaps the loneliness, once uncorked, was hard to put back in its bottle. He began asserting new needs and demands. He ventured quickly from inviting himself over to insisting that we hang out every week. I couldn't always make time, and I drew firmer boundaries. Lonely, and frustrated one day that I only stopped for the sort of quick chat that had once been our norm, he made an offhanded comment that maybe it would be better if he killed himself. Even this, maybe, was a renewed assertion of his worth. He wouldn't be content with his former isolation. I responded with thin reassurances: things were looking up; I would see him very soon.

He also gave new voice to hopes and goals. He talked about contacting his family and going home. He had an old phone number, which he wrote down for me. And though I can't say whether it was risky, it was what he wanted, so I tried to oblige. It was actually fairly simple: a quick web search suggested that Iranian phone numbers had been reformatted, and so a Farsi-speaking friend gave the old number to her cousin's wife, who gave it to her family in M.'s hometown, who were able to determine what the new number should be. More than that, they confirmed that it did, indeed, reach his family.

I felt vertiginous. I don't know how M. felt. I talked to his Iranian friend about it, who was nonplussed. (After all, he could have tried to find them, but hadn't.) His caseworker seemed nominally supportive and offered to facilitate a call but left it at that. Next, M. and I tried to make a call from my computer, late in the evening, Iranian time. We got what I guessed was an Iranian busy signal and planned to try again. But we couldn't nail down a meeting time. (He showed up a day early once, not at all another time.) And weeks passed.

And then one day, M. told me he'd contacted them himself and he was going home. I didn't believe him. I still don't. But later in the week, I called his social worker, and sure enough, he was gone. Could he have glimpsed and remembered the phone number as I dialed it? He wasn't good with numbers. Could he make international calls from the shelter? Did they buy him a ticket? If not, who did?

Or were these delusions? Or inventions? Should I have paid more heed to his offhanded comment? Should we not have even opened old wounds? I haven't tried to contact his family (yet), nor, as far as I can tell, did they try to contact me. Anyway, all I could tell them is that their son is still missing.

•   •   •

In the weeks afterward, I missed several calls from Atlanta phone numbers. When I called back, there was no answer. Atlanta is a major transit hub. Had he been stranded in the airport? Or was I being naively optimistic?

This essay is riddled with questions. Not least of them is the question so many of us ask ourselves quietly, and privately: What else could I have done? For all my critiques of the homelessness "industry," I was just as unsure of how to care best for my friend. I don't torture myself about this. I know there are not always answers. The endeavor of caring, like the endeavor of research, is built on uncertainty.

Rather than guilt, then, there is grief. Grief is more than sadness. It is care refracted through loss, but a loss to which we are not reconciled, one we can't yet assimilate within us. It clings to lost possibilities. It asks, "What if?" Grief is the pain that resists closure. And it teaches me, too, to resist closure and to care in the uncertainty. It keeps my eyes open. It stops me to talk to people I might otherwise pass by. I wonder. I doubt. I guess. I ask questions. And, hopefully, I learn. Maybe one day I'll learn what happened to M.

That was four years ago. I lived in Seattle for a further three years. I never talked to his social worker again. The Iranian restaurant changed hands. If anybody reading this knows what happened to him, please let me know.

NOTES

1. University Way Northeast, colloquially known as "The Ave," is a major arterial and commercial street that transects the University District and is located near the University of Washington in Seattle, Washington.

2. Samuel Beckett, *Waiting for Godot: Tragicomedy in Two Acts* (New York: Grove Press, 1982).

3. Martin Buber, *I and Thou*, trans. Walter Kaufmann (New York: Touchstone Press, 1996).

4. Samuel Delaney, *Times Square Red, Times Square Blue* (New York: New York University Press, 1999).

5. Judith Butler, *Frames of War: When Is Life Grievable?* (London: Verso, 2009).

6. Samira Kawash, "The Homeless Body," *Public Culture* 10, no. 2 (1998): 319–39.

7. Craig Willse, *The Value of Homelessness: Managing Surplus Life in the United States* (Minneapolis: University of Minnesota Press, 2015).

BIBLIOGRAPHY

Beckett, Samuel. *Waiting for Godot: Tragicomedy in Two Acts.* New York: Grove Press, 1982.

Buber, Martin. *I and Thou.* Translated by Walter Kaufmann. New York: Touchstone, 1996.

Butler, Judith. *Frames of War: When Is Life Grievable?* London: Verso, 2009.

Delaney, Samuel. *Times Square Red, Times Square Blue.* New York: New York University Press, 1999.

Kawash, Samira. "The Homeless Body." *Public Culture* 10, no. 2 (1998): 319–39.

Willse, Craig. *The Value of Homelessness: Managing Surplus Life in the United States.* Minneapolis: University of Minnesota Press, 2015.

CHAPTER EIGHT

Grieving Daughter, Grieving Witness

ABIGAIL H. NEELY

Having just changed into my hiking clothes, I strode into the living room, relaxed and ready to hit the trail. I had just submitted an article, and I was feeling lighter, happier, and excited to go on a long hike with my dad in the sunny Arizona winter.

As soon as I got to the middle of the room, I could tell that something had changed. My dad sat in front of the gas fireplace, completely still, staring at the pile of mail in his lap.

I walked over and asked, "Did it arrive?"

He took a deep breath and replied, "Yes," without looking up at me.

. . .

Just over three months before, I had come out of teaching a class on an unremarkable late fall afternoon to find a series of text messages and phone calls from my dad and my brothers. Walking back to my office, I called my father. He answered, crying. In disbelief, he said, "She's gone."

My mother had died. Suddenly. Unexpectedly.

I was instantly nauseated. I wanted to take back the phone call. The world around me was suddenly spinning. I wanted to run. I wanted to sleep. I wanted to cry. I wanted to fix everything. I wanted my mom.

I texted a friend to meet me at home, rushed there, gathered my things, and made the two-and-a-half-hour drive south to the Massachusetts hospital where my mom lay waiting for me.

Running into the hospital, I stopped just short of the glaring, antiseptic room where my mom, dad, brothers, and my mom's sister sat together. I called for my dad. He came out and hugged me. Drawing on his strength, I entered the room.

I'll never forget what I saw: my mother lying on a hospital bed, mouth wide open, not moving. She was there, but she was gone.

I collapsed onto the floor, my body desperate to be in the fetal position.

"No, no, no," I pleaded over and over again, with my brothers crouched down supporting either side of me.

I am no stranger to grief, death, and mourning. I do my research in rural KwaZulu-Natal, South Africa, which has one of the highest HIV and related death rates in the world.[1] In 2008 and 2009, I spent twenty months in Pholela, South Africa, conducting research for my dissertation (and I've spent many months there since). During that time, I learned a tremendous amount about health, healing, life, and the social relationships that underpinned them all, and built deep and lasting relationships with many people who live in Pholela.

One of my overwhelming memories of my dissertation research was death. It was everywhere. It was and is relentless in this place. In the three communities where I conduct research, there were two or three funerals every weekend in 2008 and

2009. And more often than not, these were funerals for young people—people between the ages of twenty and forty—who were dying at rates never before seen.[2] In retrospect, perhaps the most shocking aspect of this kind of death was how unremarkable and banal it all seemed at the time, at least in comparison to my previous experiences and my decidedly nonacademic understandings of death. In Pholela, funerals were simply a part of everyday life on the weekends, and young people dying was something everyone expected. People mourned, and a deceased person's family was visibly distraught, but the funerals felt more like rituals of necessity than moments of tremendous loss. Even for the extended family of the deceased, many of these funerals and the mourning that accompanied them were mundane. The young people who died were passing away, passing on, as though it was the most natural thing to do.

At first the everydayness of death took me by surprise. But over time, I became accustomed to it. I, like the people with whom I conduct my research, learned to survive in the face of tremendous loss by accepting it as normal, at least to a certain extent. In those years, I didn't ask many questions about death— *why* it was so common among the youth and *what* it meant for the communities I was working in—both because thinking about it would make it hurt more and because the answers seemed too haunting and too elusive. At that time, it seemed to me that death on this scale was something to survive, not something to study.

On the day I left Pholela in 2009 to return to the United States, I stopped by the home of the woman who had come to be my *gogo* (the Zulu word for "granny"). As I approached, I could hear wailing coming from the neighbor's house. Gogo Sithole (my gogo) told me that her neighbor had been killed in a car accident.[3] When I stopped by his house, his wife, Gogo Mban-jwa, was doubled over wailing, the look of shock and pain on her face seared into my memory forever.

For the first time in months, I didn't know what to do. This kind of grief was so far outside of my experience in Pholela that I just sat there, bearing witness to her pain, with no reassurances to offer beyond my presence.

For a healthy, (relatively) wealthy man in his early sixties, a sudden death like this was completely unexpected. This man had died. He had not passed away. This difference is significant. To pass away is to move on, peacefully. It is neither surprising nor shocking. In Pholela, it warrants a different, quieter, subtler kind of grief. The wailing I heard the day I visited Gogo Mban-jwa was indicative of just how sudden and significant losing her husband was. It was loud and relentless. It was devastating. It was unlike anything I had heard.

There was no mistaking that a terrible loss had occurred in this place.

In some ways, it was this kind of mourning that must have been on my mind as I collapsed onto the hospital-room floor the day my mom died. In other ways, I can only describe what happened as a bodily reaction—a need to be in the fetal position, even if it meant collapsing onto a cold hospital floor. This was a whole-body response to loss. It was not what I was used to seeing in Pholela.

As I sit here now, embarking in earnest on a new book project about death in South Africa, I am struck by how physically (and emotionally) wrecked I—and many, many people—have been by the death of my mother, and how different this is from the everydayness of much of the death and mourning that I have experienced in Pholela, especially among young adults. Death is certainly significant in Pholela, but its significance articulates differently in the rituals, grief, and mourning I have witnessed and participated in there, especially when the person lost is a young adult. Even in my earliest days of research, it was clear that death was an ever-present, if dull, force, a force different from what I expected. This new book project seeks to understand the social and material conditions that make the loss of a generation seem so mundane. It seeks to understand what death means in a place where it is both surprising and commonplace, to explore how we understand grief and mourning when it seems so different from that which my family has experienced in losing my mother—to understand *why* death is what it is in rural South Africa.

WRITING AND RESEARCHING DEATH

When I began the work of writing a book about social medicine and health and healing in Pholela from my dissertation research, I returned to the hundreds of pages of field notes I had taken between 2006 and 2012. What struck me most about those notes was how pervasive death was. It was everywhere, touching all aspects of my research and, by extension, my day-to-day life in Pholela. None of my interviews and only a couple of my participant observations had dealt directly with death, yet it was ubiquitous.

In hindsight, this seems like a rather obvious observation for a part of the world in which so many people, scholarly and otherwise, had been writing about a deadly disease for so long. But somehow it came as a surprise.

I began to think as a social scientist—as a person who seeks to understand why the world is the way it is—about what life means in a place where death and dying are pervasive and where the people dying are often young. I began to ask why. It seemed to me that this was an important and perhaps the only starting point for good, critical social science research. And so it began my next book project, on death.

As a relational thinker committed to multicausal explanations, I anticipated that I would not be searching for one answer. Instead, I figured I'd be searching for many interrelated answers to interrelated questions:[4] How did death come to affect the "youth," the people who should be the healthiest? What does this mean for communities? How and why have mourning and funerals changed? How and why have large increases in deaths changed household livelihood strategies? What has death done to family formations? Why? How does this massive epidemic of death and the concomitant shift in life expectancy affect the lives people are living? What are the global, national, local, familial, and bodily forces at work in death and dying in rural South Africa? And on and on. It became clear that this is a project with many questions that all point to a bigger question of how and why death is changing in rural South Africa, and why it matters—for the people who live there, for international organizations that are interested in the region, and for how social scientists understand health, death, and even life. Answering the question *why* would be at the center of this project.

Just six weeks before my mom died, I traveled back to Pholela to say good-bye to Gogo Sithole. Her home is my home, and she is my gogo. This was to be my first formal research trip for the new project. More important, it was a pilgrimage to say good-bye to a beloved adopted family member and to be with the people who loved her best. It was a deeply personal trip. Even then, before losing my mom, I knew that grief stitched together the personal and the collective, and for me, that it would stitch together the professional too.

Loud, long, and crowded, Gogo Sithole's funeral was a beautiful tribute to a long life well lived, one that had touched her entire community. We sang and danced, we stayed up all night. My body hurt with exhaustion, jet lag, loss. The physicality of this kind of mourning was overwhelming. People gave speeches. I gave a speech. I had never been so nervous to give a speech.

While nothing about the crowd, the ritual, and the enthusiasm of the event surprised me, I found the deep, palpable sadness of those who knew and loved Gogo Sithole best striking. Quite simply, it was the sadness that comes from permanent loss, and it was heightened by the depth of loss for the community. This was a woman who was important to so many.

I've met few people as full of life as Gogo Sithole; at her ninetieth birthday party we all remarked that we were sure she'd be around another ten years. True, she was old, older than just about everyone else in Pholela, but no one actually thought she would die. As I look back over my field notes from that funeral, the mix of somberness and celebration really sticks with me. There was more sadness at this funeral than I had seen at the others, all of which were for people much younger. Gogo Sithole's funeral, like Gogo Mbanjwa's mourning, stand out: they were more somber, more raw, more devastating, more unexpected. In Pholela, it seems, the elderly are not supposed to die.

This quick trip to Pholela for Gogo Sithole's funeral, just six weeks before I would lose my own mother, taught me much more than that the relationships between grief and loss were somewhat paradoxical in Pholela. It taught me that my research praxis would take a toll on me that I had not anticipated. A toll that I would feel physically and emotionally, a fog that would make it harder to "produce," especially when it came to writing about death. Working in the same place for more than a decade, visiting the same people, people who have become kin, means that death and grief are deeply personal for me, even as they are part of broad societal phenomena worth investigating. This proximity to death and to people—my entanglement in the social relationships of this place—all offer a depth of understanding of these losses that I would not have were I not so close to the people with whom I conduct my research. Losing my mom threw this into sharp relief, all while thickening the fog of grief.

SEARCHING FOR WHY

The day after my mom died, my dad, my brothers, and I sat around the lipstick-red pullout couch in my mother's home office to discuss whether we should get an autopsy. It felt like we were in a horrible dream—a nightmare—in which the worst thing had happened and we still had to make responsible, well-thought-out decisions.

I said I didn't care either way. But, if I'm honest, I didn't want to get one. I didn't want to find out that my mom had died from a postsurgical blood clot. I knew I'd forever be mad that she had had surgery, thinking that her knee replacement was a choice, rather than a necessity (which, of course, given quality-of-life issues, it was not). Besides, she was gone. Really, permanently gone, so what was the point? But my brothers thought the autopsy was a good idea, both because of the potential for more peace of mind for them and because it might offer some important genetic information for us. And so, we decided to get one with the hopes that knowing what caused her death might help us to understand *why* she had died.

That Arizona afternoon when I was so excited to hike, the autopsy report had arrived.

My dad and I took a deep breath, and he opened the envelope. We read the report together. Crouched over his shoulder, I scanned the document as quickly as possible to try to get to *the* answer. To try to answer the question of why my mom—a perfectly healthy seventy-two-year-old woman who was, according to just about everyone who knew her, more full of life than most twenty-five-year-olds—had died. Why she had died at all. Why she had died that October afternoon.

But the autopsy did not hold an answer. Her heart stopped. They call it dysrhythmia—an electrical storm in the heart, unpredictable and unstoppable. That was it. She was gone.

The autopsy painted a picture of what we all knew: a healthy seventy-two-year-old woman had died, and no one knew why. Her doctor told us that it was the strangest autopsy she had ever seen. "She was just so healthy," she told my dad.

As I sit here writing, three weeks after receiving the autopsy report, I am struck by how similar my experience must have been to Gogo Mbanjwa's. Her husband had died in a car crash with no explanation. He was the head of a public taxi company, and he took good care of his family. He was a man who knew his way around vehicles; he should not have died in one. He was well known and respected, just like my mom. This was sudden, as sudden as my mother's death, and it left the people he loved reeling, just as losing my mom has left me reeling. Neither I nor Gogo Mbanjwa would ever be the same again. And neither of us would ever know why.

LETTING GO OF WHY

What I learned from losing my mom and what Gogo Mbanjwa learned from losing her husband was that sometimes there is no answer to the question of why. Accidents happen, bodies behave in unexpected ways, and none of it explains why one has to lose a loved one.

The weeks since we received the autopsy report have been hard. Grief sits on me, in me, heavily. Writing through grief is an exhausting slog. It's like walking through a dense fog up a mountain with only intermittent, slight views of the path ahead. But writing also helps. It helps me understand more about losing my mom. It helps me understand more about death. In these weeks, I've begun to realize that even if we had learned that my mother had coronary artery disease and therefore that a heart attack was expected, it wouldn't have answered the question of why. Why my mom? Why now? In other words, aside from the grand truth that everyone dies, there is no answer to the question *why*.

This is a profound realization indeed, even as it is a devastating one. In South Africa, it is clear that expectations around death and dying have changed in the past twenty-five years. When a neighbor or distant relative passes away in her thirties or forties, no one is surprised; everyone takes it for granted that this is who passes away. Of course, people are sad, and those losses certainly take their toll, but there is an expectation that young people pass on. People don't ask why, because they know better. They know that HIV/AIDS, poverty, and everyday violence are not real answers. They know that there is no answer to the question *why*.

In a sense, when a country loses a generation, it adjusts, and that adjustment affects everything from rituals to family formations to grief. It doesn't ask why. Death becomes something to survive and adapt to. Something that I am slowly and painfully learning to do for myself in the wake of my gogo's death and my mother's death.

So, the challenge, as I see it, is how to do rigorous, high-quality social science that recognizes that there are no answers to the question *why*. This is particularly hard for me as a social scientist, as a person for whom asking and answering the question *why* is central to my intellectual work. Yes, I can *explain* what is happening, I can offer statistics on disease and postapartheid (un)employment, I can describe funerals and mourning, I can analyze the role of broad political-economic structures in the life and death of South Africa's poor, I can detail the changes in mourning practices and funeral rituals, and I can even describe the physical and emotional toll that loss takes on me and the people with whom I do my research. But none of this really answers the question *why*. Why are so many young people dying? Why are people so accustomed to young people dying? So the question becomes, how do we write good, critical, analytical scholarship that keeps open the possibility that we don't actually know why? That we *can't* actually know why. And that not really knowing why explains as much about the significance of death as anything else.

As I sit here now, facing the re-formation of social relationships in my own family and broader social world, I can't help wondering if perhaps we should be asking questions about relationships instead. How does the loss of a generation reconfigure the relationships that make up our social worlds? How does death reflect, refract, and reorder relationships? I don't have a complete answer yet, and I may never have one, but I think that focusing on the reconfigurations of relationships around death is a good start. To do this, I draw inspiration from the scholarship I mentioned earlier, which takes as a starting point that people and things are not bodies-unto-themselves. Instead, it shows that we exist in relation to those around us, just as they exist in relation to us. This scholarship posits that we are all relational beings, constantly forming and re-forming through our entanglements with each other. Instead of asking *why* people die—individuals and generations—perhaps we should be asking how loss leads to a reconfiguration of the multiple worlds we inhabit.

Losing my mom has taught me that sometimes the most deep and profound things in life—and, by extension, in society—offer no answer to the question *why*. As my family and the communities who love my mom best work to navigate a new and unruly sea of social relationships without her, I know in my bones that these reconfigurations matter and that they offer to teach us much about the social worlds we inhabit and how death and life affect them. Losing my mom, losing my gogo, and sharing the grief of my family, friends, and the communities in which I live and do my research have taught me much about death, even as I have much to learn. One of the most important lessons is that bearing witness—experiencing and surviving loss—is fundamental to researching, to understanding death and life, even if it makes it harder to write, and even if we'll never fully understand why.

NOTES

1. Avert, an organization dedicated to collecting and disseminating information on HIV/AIDS, puts the prevalence rate in KwaZulu-Natal at 40 percent; this compares with 26 percent in Swaziland, the country with the highest rate in the world. Avert, "HIV/AIDS in South Africa," accessed December 4, 2017, www.avert.org/professionals/hiv-around-world/sub-saharan-africa/south-africa.

2. The popular scholar imagines that these deaths are attributable to HIV/AIDS. In my time in Pholela, I have found the picture to be more complicated. This epidemic of death among the youth is related to more diseases than just HIV/AIDS; diseases like TB, diabetes, and hypertension, as well as accidents and violent crime, have significant impacts on death rates among the youth.

3. In accordance with human subjects ethics review requirements, all names of people in South Africa are pseudonyms.

4. I take particular inspiration from work of feminist science studies scholars who focus on entanglements, understanding the world as the product of relationships and questioning the notion that individual bodies exist outside of their relationships with others. Annemarie Mol and John Law have written much about understanding bodies as relational through an actor-network theory framework. Donna Haraway has long enlightened us about nature-society relationships through a relational understanding. Her most recent work on companion species pushes us to think about these relationships at the bodily scale, which offers much for understanding the bodily implications of grief. I take particular inspiration from Karen Barad, who, drawing on Giles Deleuze and Félix Guattari, posits that humans and nonhumans come into being through their relationships with one another. I am also inspired by a number of feminist geographers, including Cindi Katz, Gillian Rose, Farhana Sultana, and Juanita Sundberg, among others, who write about the importance of the relationships that underpin their research, between themselves and collaborators and between themselves and research participants. These scholars reveal that these relationships are fundamental to their work. See, particularly, Karen Barad, "Posthumanist Performativity: Toward an Understanding of How Matter Comes to Matter," *Signs* 28, no. 3 (2003): 801–31; Karen Barad, *Meeting the Universe Halfway: Quantum Physics and the Entanglement of Matter and Meaning* (Durham, NC: Duke University Press, 2007); Donna Haraway, *Simians, Cyborgs, and Women: The Reinvention of Nature* (New York: Routledge, 1991); Donna Haraway, *When Species Meet* (Minneapolis: University of Minnesota Press, 2008); Cindi Katz, "Playing the Field: Questions of Fieldwork in Geography," *Professional Geographer* 46, no. 1 (1994): 67–72; John Law and Annemarie Mol, "Notes on Materiality and Sociality," *Sociological Review* 43, no. 2

(1995): 274–94; Annemarie Mol and John Law, "Embodied Action, Enacted Bodies: The Example of Hypoglycaemia," *Body and Society* 10, no. 2–3 (2004): 43–62; Abigail Neely and Thokozile Nguse, "Entanglements, Intra-actions, and Diffraction," in *The Routledge Handbook of Political Ecology*, edited by Tom Perreault, Gavin Bridge, and James McCarthy (London: Routledge, 2015), 140–51; Gillian Rose, "Situating Knowledges: Positionality, Reflexivities and Other Tactics," *Progress in Human Geography* 21, no. 3 (1997): 305–20; Farhana Sultana, "Reflexivity, Positionality and Participatory Ethics: Negotiating Fieldwork Dilemmas in International Research," *ACME: An International E-Journal for Critical Geographies* 6, no. 3 (2007): 374–84; Juanita Sundberg, "Masculinist Epistemologies and the Politics of Fieldwork in Latin Americanist Geography," *Professional Geographer* 55, no. 2 (2003), 180–90; Juanita Sundberg, "Ethics, Entanglement and Political Ecology," in *The Routledge Handbook of Political Ecology*, edited by Tom Perreault, Gavin Bridge, and James McCarthy (London: Routledge, 2015), 127–40.

BIBLIOGRAPHY

Avert. "HIV/Aids in South Africa." Accessed December 4, 2017. www .avert.org/professionals/hiv-around-world/sub-saharan-africa/south -africa.

Barad, Karen. *Meeting the Universe Halfway: Quantum Physics and the Entanglement of Matter and Meaning.* Durham, NC: Duke University Press, 2007.

———. "Posthumanist Performativity: Toward an Understanding of How Matter Comes to Matter." *Signs* 28, no. 3 (2003): 801–31.

Haraway, Donna. *Simians, Cyborgs, and Women: The Reinvention of Nature.* New York: Routledge, 1991.

———. *When Species Meet.* Minneapolis: University of Minnesota Press, 2008.

Katz, Cindi. "Playing the Field: Questions of Fieldwork in Geography." *Professional Geographer* 46, no. 1 (1994): 67–72.

Law, John, and Annemarie Mol. "Notes on Materiality and Sociality." *Sociological Review* 43, no. 2 (1995): 274–94.

Mol, Annemarie, and John Law. "Embodied Action, Enacted Bodies: The Example of Hypoglycaemia." *Body and Society* 10, no. 2–3 (2004): 43–62.

Neely, Abigail, and Thokozile Nguse. "Entanglements, Intra-actions, and Diffraction." In *The Routledge Handbook of Political Ecology*, edited by Tom Perreault, Gavin Bridge, and James McCarthy, 140–51. London: Routledge, 2015.

Rose, Gillian. "Situating Knowledges: Positionality, Reflexivities and Other Tactics." *Progress in Human Geography* 21, no. 3 (1997): 305–20.

Sultana, Farhana. "Reflexivity, Positionality and Participatory Ethics: Negotiating Fieldwork Dilemmas in International Research." *ACME: An International E-Journal for Critical Geographies* 6, no. 3 (2007): 374–85.

Sundberg, Juanita. "Ethics, Entanglement and Political Ecology." In *The Routledge Handbook of Political Ecology*, edited by Tom Perreault, Gavin Bridge, and James McCarthy, 127–40. London: Routledge, 2015.

———. "Masculinist Epistemologies and the Politics of Fieldwork in Latin Americanist Geography." *Professional Geographer* 55, no. 2 (2003): 180–90.

CHAPTER NINE

The Researcher-Witness of Violence against Queers

One Scholar-Activist's Pathway through Lament

WILLIAM J. PAYNE

ALMENDRA (ALMOND): HER NAME SHALL NOT BE FORGOTTEN

Chilpancingo, Mexico. June 9, 2012. I was in a restaurant with a group of queer activists. A pizza parlor. It was my third visit to this city, the capital of the state of Guerrero in the southern part of the country. The goal of the trip was to conduct preliminary research for a project focused on the human rights of sexual and gender minorities in a place facing high levels of violence and impunity.[1]

The activists had just organized a series of events focused on LGBTI rights, a "cultural week" dedicated to the memory of a gay community leader named Quetzalcoatl Leija. A year earlier, in a crime that remains unsolved, someone had beaten Leija to death in a laneway, just steps from the cathedral in the center of town. As we ate and reminisced about the week's events, I remember that spirits were high because of an excellent turnout and an especially powerful annual pride march (the eleventh for the town). Then, one of the activists received a phone call: the lifeless body of a young trans woman had been discovered on the edge of town. A few minutes later I found myself on the way to the city morgue.

Almost as if by rote, the activists knew what that moment required of them. The authorities had not yet identified the deceased, and the activists saw it as their duty to make sure her loved ones learned of her death as soon as possible. Before all else, her death must be mourned. The coroner showed us a series of high-resolution images of the deceased woman, whose lifeless body was laid out in the next room. The coroner described her: "Slim, 1.66 meters, shoe size 24, long hair, no makeup on face, second toe longer than the big toe, keloid scar on her right knee that looks like a star, light brown skin, brown eyes, straight medium-sized nose, regular mouth and lips, dressed in Lycra (zebra print, white and black), toenails poorly maintained." (The coroner said this indicates poverty.) Her body was found in a ravine, wrapped in plastic bags and a piece of green fabric. No one recognized her. One of the activists took photos of the images to send to a listserv they managed. I would later learn that the woman's preferred name was Almendra, which means "almond."

As is the case with most of the thousands of murders that have taken place over the past decade in Guerrero, no one has been charged in relation to Almendra's death. Days after her eighteenth birthday, and at the height of pride season, during which towns and cities across that state held their own celebrations of sexual and gender diversity, Almendra's life was ended in ignominious obscurity. Through my research, I have intimate knowledge of Almendra's childhood, adolescence, and final days, and how all were punctuated by violence of various forms. I know things that I cannot report here because the information could compromise my sources. The writing up of sensitive research can be a perplexing task, as the commitment to anonymity and confidentiality means that key information that helps make sense of particular circumstances must be obfuscated, veiled, anonymized, oftentimes detached from the specific case, and sometimes left unsaid. What does one do with the grief that this leaves pitted in one's stomach?

The process of interviewing has made me a secondary witness to suffering. This research exposes me to informants' experiences of grieving and compels me to grieve with them. In 2015, the editors of this book organized two panels at the annual meeting of the American Association of Geographers entitled "Grieving Witnesses: The Politics of Grief in the Field." As I was preparing my notes to speak about this matter of the relationship between grief and research, I realized I had forgotten Almendra's name. This was confusing and left me feeling like I was in danger of losing sight of something fundamental to this work. Stories like Almendra's had brought me to the academy. After more than a decade of solidarity work with marginalized communities as part of horizontally structured organizations, I arrived late to graduate school to find responses to my unanswered questions regarding the violence I had witnessed, and to begin to explore the identity of scholar-activist. My master's and doctoral projects emerged out of experiences of being a human rights worker in armed conflict zones as a queer-identified person. I have taken down the details of dozens of stories like Almendra's, in Colombia, in Mexico, and elsewhere.

Too often, though, the very stories that brought me to the academy in the first place seem to recede into the background, to mutate into a functional element of the process of "doing research." The stories simply become data. Sometimes, it seems that my location in the academy itself makes it difficult to actually *do something*. I am left wondering about the limits of being an academic. Too often, I have found it easy to paper over the jumble of emotions tied to this research.

In this chapter, I reflect on my experience, on my own encounter with human suffering, and with that morass of feelings we call grief in relation to such tragedy. I reflect on where it has taken me as a researcher and as a political subject, and on what it means when I find that I do not lament some deaths, that their suffering becomes somehow acceptable. Central to this reflection, I seek to pay attention to the privilege I experience that enables me to sometimes forget and pay attention to the limits of scholar-activism.

ALVARO AND BOBBY: THE KILLING OF RESEARCH SUBJECTS

Death is a thief in the night. Often, he surprises his prey even when his arrival might have been foreseen. My research involves a close look at queer and trans folk whose lives have been cut short in contexts marked by political violence and impunity. At times, my fieldwork has led to unanticipated close encounters with death and his cohort.

As a proxy witness to violence, suffering, and injustice through research, I am left to wonder what to do with the jumble of emotions that seem so unimportant in the face of such harm, and yet remain mine to figure out as I navigate my role as researcher. The masking of emotions is a common part of the world of academia—especially for those already marginalized by gender, race, class, and other markers of identity. However, this act of masking does not in fact erase the emotions in question and often leads to "emotional spill-out" that can either reproduce existing hierarchies or be leveraged in opposition to the status quo.[2] The task at hand is to ensure that as critical scholars we politicize our very real feelings of confusion, sadness, and grief in favor of a less violent world.

Twice, I learned that people who had provided useful insight into the dynamics of this violence, as well as productive connections to other informants, were themselves subsequently brutally murdered. In one case, a community vocally mourned the death of one of its own and denounced the tragic loss of life of yet another queer sibling; in the other case, those who knew the man—someone from Canada who had retired to Mexico—dismissed his death as the unsurprising progression of the choices he had made and seemed to give him no further thought. A clear difference between these two individuals was that people recognized the former as connected to them in a shared experience of discrimination and threat of harm; in contrast, the latter relied on his privileged position for protection from possible danger associated with being a sexual minority and thus failed to represent the position of someone who had suffered because of homophobia.

Alvaro Miguel Rivera, an important Colombian queer activist, was one of these people who provided key support to my field research and was subsequently killed. A mutual friend had connected us, and in July 2005 Alvaro hosted me for my first visit to the city of Cali, the principal urban center in southwestern Colombia. Upon my arrival, we sat together in his living room, where he briefed me on the links between illegal armed groups and homo/lesbi/transphobic violence in Colombia.[3]

Alvaro informed me of a series of murders of trans people on the streets of Cali, perpetrated by elements of organized crime; at least one such case per month was occurring at that point in time: "They drive down the street in armored vehicles, and when they come across a trans woman they grab her, shoot her ... and then dump her ..."

"Why?" I asked, incredulous.

"Simple hate. Nothing more."

Alvaro lamented that the city's government was marked by homophobia and refused to respond to this wave of violence, a pattern of complicity and impunity I would come to understand in painful detail in a subsequent research project there. On the evening of my first day in Cali, Alvaro showed me the sites of queer Cali and later put me in touch with others who knew firsthand how Colombia's long-standing civil war mapped onto the bodies of sexual and gender dissidents. We stayed in touch, although the correspondence was thinner than I would prefer to admit. Three years later, a friend called from Colombia and told me that Alvaro had been bludgeoned to death in his home the night before. I remember in vivid detail how I sat in front of my computer on the other side of the world and watched a newsreel that showed Alvaro's shrouded body being carried to a useless ambulance.[4]

Then, in early 2014, I learned that a key informant for my research on violence and the LGBTI sector in Guerrero had also been killed. By happenstance, I had first met Bobby the previous year in Acapulco while grabbing a bite at a beachfront hamburger joint.[5] A tall, thin man with blond (bleached?) hair and a neatly trimmed pencil-thin mustache that contrasted oddly with fingernails that merited a good scrub and trim, by all accounts he was probably in his late sixties, though no one seemed to know for sure and Bobby remained mum on the point. Three years earlier, after visiting regularly for nearly two decades, he had sold his property in a midsize city in Canada and began to live full-time in this Mexican port. Bobby was one of the hundreds of older foreigners, mostly from Canada and the United States, who had eschewed trendier retirement destinations elsewhere in Mexico and had opted to make this dilapidated resort town long past its prime their home in exile. He gave me the lay of the land, so to speak, and put me in touch with several key informants who helped me understand earlier chapters of Acapulco's history, one that was formed in the crucible of a toxic mix of international tourism and desperate poverty that had resulted in widespread sexual exploitation of children and youth, and was punctuated by a US government operation against Americans in Acapulco that resulted in several arrests by 2002. Bobby said that this enforcement activity, in which Mexican authorities also participated, pushed such activities further underground or elsewhere.

A few months after my initial contact with Bobby, I returned to Acapulco to follow up on some of the threads from my previous research there. Another informant told me that Bobby had been killed. Reportedly, four young men—including at least two minors as well as Bobby's young adult "boyfriend"—had been staying at his home and were involved in his death. He was killed by blunt force trauma, a bottle smashed over his head. The shards were then used to stab him in the face and chest, though the forensic report suggests that he was already dead from the initial blow. Bobby had mentioned a "boyfriend" to me, a young man he also paid as a live-in housekeeper. News accounts repeated the contention of the police that it was a "crime of passion." Three of the accused were later arrested in possession of some of Bobby's property. The fourth suspect died while fleeing the police under what remain hazy circumstances that may or may not have included a fall from a roof and gunfire (the news reports are contradictory).

GRIEF AS A POLITICAL ACT

On the sixth anniversary of Alvaro's death—and amid negotiations between the government and the country's largest guerrilla group—the LGBTI rights organization Colombia Diversa paid homage to his human rights work and repeated its long lament that the state has failed to properly investigate his murder: "Alvaro Miguel Rivera was a passionate defender of human rights ... and was our friend. Sadly, the crime committed against him remains in impunity.... Today and always we remember him with the pain produced by a country that continues to persecute those who dream of a better Colombia."[6] Even as he stumbled, Alvaro passed on the baton. In Susan Sontag's reflection on those whose untimely demise comes through senseless violence, she reminds us that "these dead are supremely uninterested in the living ... in those who took their lives; in witnesses."[7] Rather, it is those who are living who need to remember, to memorialize, and to create meaning out of the suffering of those who have passed away.

Sontag also proposes that the right to look at suffering depends on the capacity to do something about it, or at the very least to learn from it. Considered individually and together, these vignettes speak to the turmoil that research of violence borne of marginalization implies. The jumble of feelings cannot be simply set aside. It may be that the dead are indifferent to our actions, yet we need to contemplate what it means when we find ourselves veering toward indifference. The story of Bobby points to the disintegration that results from the impunity that so often marks the social configurations wrought by that strange formation that is the state in these modern times. The stories of Almendra and Alvaro show how community sometimes resists that impunity. Taken together, these stories remind us that as researchers we should not seek the license granted the detached objective scientist, that ghost of positivism that continues to haunt our scholarly endeavors, but instead allow the ferment of those lives that touch us through research to reshape our intellectual query.

Perhaps it is in the decision to make our grief a political act, to lament that Almendra never had much of a chance because of the choices of others, to refuse to let Alvaro's name be forgotten, and to remember that the harm that clung to Bobby's life and death was not inevitable, that it is through such a posture that we find the compass that points the way forward in dealing with violence, suffering, and injustice.

To bring such a stance to research is a dimension of what has come to be called scholar-activism. Paul Routledge and Kate Driscoll Derickson lament that "efforts by researchers to situate themselves in relation to their research have too often focused on the individual researcher's positionality rather than on structural relationships that mediate those positionalities."[8] And they call us to a research practice that is intensely relational, that is informed by both our core values and our feelings, and that is aimed not so much at the production of knowledge but rather at social transformation. In her exploration of what she calls the "hyphenated life," Audrey Williams June says that scholar-activists "must be ready to fend off the perception that their activism taints their scholarship."[9] Despite the very real constraints, the academy does provide us with tools and with co-travelers who aid us on the journey of enacting social change in the face of the sort of horrific violence that marks our world, to remember the stories we have been told in such a way that the memory is part of transformative action.

ACKNOWLEDGMENTS

I am so grateful to the numerous LGBTI activists in Colombia and Mexico who have agreed to share their stories with me. The world is a better place because of their work.

NOTES

1. As the violence in Mexico's Guerrero State has dramatically increased over the past decade, so too has the reach of Canadian mining companies. And while this is a different dimension of the larger story than the one I seek to tell in this chapter, I mention it as a reminder that places are not naturally violent, but rather violence becomes rooted in places for a host of interrelated reasons. And perhaps also because I too come from Canada.

2. Fem-Mentee Collective: Alison L. Bain, Rachael Baker, Nicole Laliberté, Alison Milan, William J. Payne, Léa Ravensbergen, and Dima Saad, "Emotional Masking and Spill-outs in the Neoliberalized University: A Feminist Geographic Perspective on Mentorship," *Journal of Geography in Higher Education* 41, no. 4 (2017): 1–18.

3. William Payne, "Death-Squads Contemplating Queers as Citizens: What Colombian Paramilitaries Are Saying," *Gender, Place and Culture* 23, no. 3 (2016): 328–44.

4. The long-standing armed conflict in Colombia is also incomprehensible without a consideration of its transnational dimensions, the history of colonial and neocolonial expressions of power that has continuously depleted its social structures. My cynicism suggests that it is premature to celebrate recent apparent advances in negotiating a

solution to the long-standing dispute given that the same international community that is cocked to extol the apparent progress also pounces on every opportunity to exploit this country's natural resources with barely a glance toward the needs of its tenants. Violence is always productive.

5. "Bobby" is a pseudonym. I have also fictionalized aspects of the accounts of their and others' stories.

6. Colombia Diversa, "Se cumplen seis años del asesinato de Álvaro Miguel Rivera" (blog), March 6, 2015, www.colombia-diversa.org/2015/03/se-cumplen-seis-anos-del-asesinato-de.html.

7. Susan Sontag, *Regarding the Pain of Others* (New York: Picador, 2003), 125.

8. Paul Routledge and Kate Driscoll Derickson, "Situated Solidarities and the Practice of Scholar-Activism," *Environment and Planning D: Society and Space* 33, no. 3 (2015): 392.

9. Audrey Williams June, "When Activism Is Worth the Risk," *Chronicle of Higher Education*, July 20, 2015.

BIBLIOGRAPHY

Fem-Mentee Collective: Alison L. Bain, Rachael Baker, Nicole Laliberté, Alison Milan, William J. Payne, Léa Ravensbergen, and Dima Saad. "Emotional Masking and Spill-outs in the Neoliberalized University: A Feminist Geographic Perspective on Mentorship." *Journal of Geography in Higher Education* 41, no. 4 (2017): 1–18.

Payne, William. "Death-Squads Contemplating Queers as Citizens: What Colombian Paramilitaries Are Saying." *Gender, Place and Culture* 23, no. 3 (2016): 328–44.

Routledge, Paul, and Kate Driscoll Derickson. "Situated Solidarities and the Practice of Scholar-Activism." *Environment and Planning D: Society and Space* 33, no. 3 (2015): 391–407.

Sontag, Susan. *Regarding the Pain of Others.* New York: Picador, 2003.

Williams June, Audrey. "When Activism Is Worth the Risk." *Chronicle of Higher Education*, July 20, 2015.

CHAPTER TEN

Unsteady Hands

Care and Grief for Conservation Subjects

JENNY R. ISAACS

EX SITU

Holding the large Madagascar hissing cockroach was the hardest part of my summer training at the zoo. I delayed it for weeks. I recoiled from what I saw as huge, ugly, brown-armored creatures with too many legs—how could I let one of these crawl on me? Embarrassed, I hid my hesitation: since swooning and revulsion were unacceptable reactions for a serious zoo educator. In training, we were disciplined to neither "talk down" to animals nor show affection by calling any animal "cute" or speaking to them in falsetto "like they were babies." The day of contact inevitably came. I warned the other fellows that I might puke, pass out, or both. I held my breath and opened the Tupperware carrying container, then scooped the roach off his paper towel bed. Blanching, I let the animal probe me with his long antennae while, terrified and sweating, I tripped over a rehearsed recitation of his natural history. Then I unexpectedly grew calm and curious about this individual; I wondered, what was he thinking about this encounter, was he scared too? I stopped sweating. Then, after a few moments, I asked how to tell them apart, which was which? Or rather, who was who? Overcoming my fear, I felt surprised to be told with ambivalence, "Just make up some names. We go through a lot of these. They don't live very long." Hearing that, something shifted: I wasn't scared of the roach anymore, I felt angry on his behalf.

Not long after, we lost a cockroach. During a demo, the animal leaped out of my hand and scuttered across the rainbow-colored rug. The children jumped back squealing, and I fumbled to catch him as he ran. A girl stomped her foot—she managed to stop the roach, but he was injured. I was careful not to overreact, for fear of shaming the girl. But upon close inspection of the insect, I noticed a bent antenna as well as a gray plasma-like substance leaking from a hole in his abdomen. Hiding my concern, I rushed through the lesson. After the demonstration, my mentor took the animal back to the cockroach tank. I inquired nervously what might happen to him—could he be saved? "Probably not." I was visibly filled with guilt. Kindly trying to alleviate my suffering, she comforted me, saying, "Hey, they're just bugs. Don't worry about it." I looked down at him, oozing. I felt the guilt mix with anger, yet I said nothing. My sense of relation to these insects had changed from being afraid and thinking they're gross, to a sense of curiosity that sparked first concern, then anger, and finally, grief. The roaches' disposability struck me as sad: they were not given "real names" because no one bothered to recognize their forced sacrifice as species representatives—quite the opposite, they were interchangeable, anonymous, and therefore ungrievable.

IN SITU

Before dawn, we set the nets and walked the transect across the marsh, in sight of New York City just across the Hudson River. After corralling the migratory songbirds into our nets, we started the first collection round beneath the power lines adjacent to Interstate 95. At net two, I tried to calm the tech in training as we spotted more than two dozen struggling birds,

"It'll be okay, but we have to hurry." I reminded him to focus only on the bird in his hand: freeing first the right wing, then the left wing, head, then legs. I worked to free a male redstart, a sparrow-sized migratory bird, who thrashed as I tried to untangle him, turning him over and over, passing him between hands, peeling back layers of stubborn twine with my finger-less gloves. "Stop moving, bird!" I yelled, but he writhed and twisted himself deeper into knots, his eyes wide, bill open, and heart racing. The tech yelled, "Look at this! I think something already got to these ones!" I ran over and saw several bleeding and shredded birds, dangling at the bottom row of our net, many decapitated or gutted. "What happened?!" the tech asked. I explained that while these birds were struggling in the net, they were torn apart by one of the feral cats who patrolled our nets. "I think this bird might still be alive! What should I do?!" he replied, blood on his hands. "Hold on!" I yelled back. My heart raced; emotion flooded my practice. As I worked faster, my bird struggled harder. Sensing the opportunity for escape, he pulled hard toward the sky; still holding his leg between my thumb and forefinger, I felt it quietly snap, like a toothpick. There was no cry from the bird, but I muttered, "Oh no . . ." My hands fell limp, and I absently let him fly off. I was stunned with horror and grief, imagining that the tiny bird would soon most likely die under these buzzing power lines, abandoned by his flock, because of my unsteady hands. I radioed my boss and confessed what happened, fighting back tears. He curtly told me to "cut it out" adding, "When you get emotional, birds die." We worked for hours more, removing birds in a triage sequence: the rarest, bleeding, and smallest of birds "processed" first, then bigger birds, with the most common sparrows processed last. Some birds waited for us to free them for an hour, in the nets or in handmade, cotton drawstring bags hung on a modified coat rack that twitched in disturbing animation as the birds inside flailed blindly for freedom. After the hectic pace of the day, I realized that unlike those weighed, measured, tagged, and released at the processing station, the bird I injured, and those others killed in the net that day, were not given

US Geological Survey numbers and recorded. The deaths of these individuals, who lost their lives for our research, did not even register in the data. Effectively, their lives and deaths (and my accompanying concern and grief for them) were rendered illegible. I volunteered often at the site, motivated by conflicting yet related feelings of both love and grief. While I love contact with wild birds and studying them in situ, I was determined to help as many individuals as possible quickly escape from our nets without permanent harm.

. . .

In both of these settings, animal lives and deaths were literally in our hands. Each day in the field, across these and other sites, in the course of saving species, individual animal suffering is tolerated as regretfully necessary by those within the exclusive conservation community—those who are in a direct position to protect or free their conservation subjects. Conversely, expressions of pleasure and affinity toward animal subjects are discouraged and muted, confined to stolen moments (a rushed photo op of a bird-in-hand at the banding site or a quick kiss or pat on the fur of a "demonstration animal" while placing them back in their cage for the day). In these contexts, though multispecies intimacy is the daily norm, there is an expected performance of objectivity on the part of conservation professionals that restricts the expression of emotion, repressing experiences of grief and/or delight.

For many reasons, this hands-on or "applied" conservation work dedicated to saving nonhuman life requires the emotional labor of detached engagement in practice, challenging the definition of "care." Here I ask: By what logics do conservation professionals accept this conflicted status quo, and does it make us well-meaning monsters? What are the rules governing where, when, and how it is permissible for conservation professionals to have and express emotion? Might ambivalence and suppression of grief or delight be a distorted expression or form of care and even love? How might conservation be improved through more open exchanges of grief and love?

My purpose here is not to scorn applied conservation as insensitive or conservationists as cold or cruel. Yes, I write to recognize the unknown, ungrieved animals whose lives were fully spent (or taken) for science. I write as well as a gesture to other conservation practitioners and researchers who are also struggling with difficult, contradictory emotions in their work. The task of suppressing emotions is noteworthy because it hints at a disciplinary power that operates through the body. Focusing on discomfort, on the surprising affect and spontaneous emotional responses that both motivate and are produced and conditioned by conservation work, is radical as it challenges the normative mission of saving species and the positioning of conservationists as always-virtuous heroes. I add my voice to the chorus of other writers who argue that it is time to critically examine the ethical paradox at the heart of conservation.[1] In so doing, I hope conservation may be more successful and more humane.

The foundations of conservation are emotional, normatively motivated by a permissible type of love and grief. Conservation can be viewed as an exercise motivated by a love of wild places and beings, with specific goals for recovery revealing judgments about an ideal natural state. Foundational thinkers Michael E. Soule and Bruce Wilcox describe conservation biology as "mission-driven," and Edward O. Wilson describes it as a "discipline with a deadline" and an "intensive-care ward of ecology."[2] For conservationists working in the context of the Anthropocene, this foundational grief is upscaled, and the mission to conserve has been made epic. Conservation work is now described in planetary, geological, and historical terms with enormous stakes, increasingly viewed as an uphill or losing battle, where many already mourn "the end of nature."[3] Illustrating how this resembles the denial stage of grief at an exponential scale, Jamie Lorimer writes that "for some ... the magnitude and consequences of our geological entanglements are proving hard to accept."[4] Desperate responses proliferate: resignation; dramatic upscaling of protection measures; radical "new conservation" schemes such as mass translocation of animal refugees reviving extinct or cloning species; and geo-engineering proposals.[5] Within this crisis or "triage" context, under a managerial gaze, certain nonhumans and places are labeled as more deserving of immediate and intensive care (and grief) than others.

To meet its mission, conservation biologists set targets for species viability at the population level. The health of biodiversity is represented and measured within three abstract tiers— genes, species, and ecosystems—and the priorities of conservation are equally abstract, measured over large quantitative blocks of time or in percentages, for instance, rates of change over years and decades, increase or decrease in large population sizes.[6] Using such calculations, individual lives are not, and have never been, the central concern of conservation.[7] In Krithika Srinivasan's words, "The individual becomes chiefly a means to an end" in a context where "an entanglement of harm and care goes with the sacrificial logic of population: individuals can be harmfully intervened on in the name of universal wellbeing."[8] When the whole planet is in trouble, each death is made small, and in some cases even deemed necessary. Acceptable grief then is reserved for an imagined more-pristine past, and in specific response to scientifically defined species extinction crises. Grief at the large scale then allows for the reproduction of practices that accept that individual animals may suffer or die (accidentally, incidentally) as the result of well-intentioned research so that masses of anonymous/future others might potentially recover. Despite conservation's depersonalized positioning and abstract organizing logic, species are still going extinct exponentially faster than the normal background rate per thousand species.

To improve this work, for all involved, I urge conservation practitioners to keep their focus on the animal in their hands and to embrace their role as caregivers. Expressions of care, including grief or delight, on the event level are fully consistent with the logic of care and the caring motivations that inspire wildlife species conservation at the species or planetary level. In fact, rather than in opposition to it, and beyond being appropriate, caring is essential for conservation to meet its mission. If it is to succeed, Kyle Van Houtan insists that conservation must be tied to emotion, specifically in despair/hope, since "hope lies amidst despair." He explains, "To succeed as a social cause, conservation needs a hope that academic science itself cannot provide. Conservation needs a cultural legitimacy that inspires enthusiasm, allegiance, and personal sacrifice—in other words, actual changes in human behavior."[9] Instead of pretending we don't have deep emotional responses to the species we study in the field, or repressing our sorrow for their suffering, expressing affinity with our conservation subjects can serve as a powerful form of conservation leadership by example. By excusing ourselves from the need to perform the role of impartial scientist and by resolving conservation contradictions around grief and caring across scales, we find the potential to dissipate much of the suffering and contortion experienced by both conservation captor and captive. Such attention to the mobilizing as well as harmful role of grief in applied conservation exposes its logical inconsistencies, politicizes interspecies encounters, and pushes conservation toward more benign, individualized management approaches.[10] These may be more time and resource intensive, but they also hold the promise to work more humanely for all participants.

I still band sometimes. The truth is I miss birds when I'm away from the field. But I stay away more than not, as I am haunted by the memories of handling scared, dead, and dying birds. Of the tiniest birds having heart attacks as I raced them back to the station, holding them under my shirt against my heart to keep them warm. Of wet birds being blown in the wind like strings of broken Christmas lights in the cold, October rain. Of the fierce, relentless bite of a male cardinal attached to my finger, determined to be free yet not letting go. I remember many others unable to fly—hopping away with wing strain, dying in a shoe box, or those who remained close by, huddled and shaking under our table. I carry these bright memories— these trespasses—as a burden. Having held them in my hands, I feel a responsibility to each bird individually, and I dare not return without a sober understanding that while contact between species can be thrilling, such a thrill always comes with a cost.

I sometimes go back to the zoo, now with my children or students, and I share personal stories of the times when those animals were in my hands, up close. Their eyes sparkle as they imagine such encounters and fantasize about working at the zoo. During my summer there, through daily interactions in the classroom or gazing through the thick glass of animal enclosures, my enthusiasm for being close to the zoo's "wild" residents and playing the role of conservation hero steadily waned, sinking into dull, multifolded grief. It wasn't just grief for the anonymous cockroaches, lizards, or tank frogs whose subjective experiences, lives, and deaths failed to spark much human interest. Like many visitors, I grieved for the charismatic celebrity "ambassador" animals, pampered and beloved, yet restricted in their movements, with artificial social-ecological lives, far away from their "natural" environments. I felt grief over the destruction of their habitats, for the violences and social structures that created such a place, enabling this captor-captive relationship, and my role in continuing it. I grieved over my naive, uncritical willingness to reproduce such an uneven status quo.

My affinity for nonhuman life motivates my work and still animates my time in the field. I share these stories and emotions with other conservationists who also care for nature and may be wrestling with similar misgivings. As I finish this, holding onto nothing but memories of encounters with exotic cockroaches and bright birds, I grieve for my possible future without animals in it—for the career in conservation fieldwork I might be damaging by writing this—and hope that conservation might be a safer place for practitioners to freely express their love and grief. I offer my experiences as a respectful opening for dialogue, as a means to stand with those who desperately need us to provide a more caring model of conservation.

NOTES

1. Marc Bekoff, ed., *Ignoring Nature No More: The Case for Compassionate Conservation* (Chicago: University of Chicago Press, 2013).

2. Michael E. Soule and Bruce A. Wilcox, *Conservation Biology: An Evolutionary-Ecological Perspective* (Sunderland, MA: Sinauer, 1980); Edward O. Wilson, "Editorial: On the Future of Conservation Biology," *Conservation Biology* 14, no. 1 (2000): 1–3.

3. Bill McKibben, *The End of Nature* (New York: Random House, 1989). See also Richard J. Hobbs, "Grieving for the Past and Hoping for the Future: Balancing Polarizing Perspectives in Conservation and Restoration," *Restoration Ecology* 21, no. 2 (2013): 141–48.

4. Jamie Lorimer *Wildlife in the Anthropocene* (Minneapolis: University of Minnesota Press, 2015), 1.

5. Edward O. Wilson, *Half-Earth: Our Planet's Fight for Fife* (New York: W. W. Norton, 2016); Josh Donlan, "Re-wilding North America," *Nature* 436, no. 7053 (2005): 913–14.

6. For example, see the International Union for Conservation of Nature Red List classification system of conservation status: www.iucnredlist.org/technical-documents/classification-schemes.

7. On Foucault's biopower and the relationship between ontological scale/politics, "acceptable harm," and "agential subjectification," see Krithika Srinivasan, "Caring for the Collective: Biopower and Agential Subjectification in Wildlife Conservation," *Environment and Planning D: Society and Space* 32, no. 3 (2014): 501–17; see also Michael Hutchins and Christen Wemmer, "Wildlife Conservation and Animal Rights: Are They Compatible?," in *Advances in Animal Welfare Science 1986/1987*, ed. Michael W. Fox and Linda D. Mickley (Boston: Martinus Nijhoff, 1987), 111–37.

8. Srinivasan, "Caring for the Collective," 506.

9. Kyle S. Van Houtan, "Conservation as Virtue: A Scientific and Social Process for Conservation Ethics," *Conservation Biology* 20, no. 5 (2006), 1367–72.

10. For instance, passive wildlife management methods, such as photo identification (e.g., whales) by skin pattern instead of tagging, or management of human-animal conflict through individualized monitoring and familiarity (e.g., with particularly troublesome elephants or rhinos).

BIBLIOGRAPHY

Bekoff, Marc, ed. *Ignoring Nature No More: The Case for Compassionate Conservation*. Chicago: University of Chicago Press, 2013.

Donlan, Josh. "Re-wilding North America." *Nature* 436, no. 7053 (2005): 913–14.

Hobbs, Richard J. "Grieving for the Past and Hoping for the Future: Balancing Polarizing Perspectives in Conservation and Restoration." *Restoration Ecology* 21, no. 2 (2013): 145–48.

Hutchins, Michael, and Christen Wemmer. "Wildlife Conservation and Animal Rights: Are They Compatible?" In *Advances in Animal Welfare Science 1986/1987*, edited by Michael W. Fox and Linda D. Mickley, 111–37. Boston: Martinus Nijhoff, 1987.

Lorimer, Jamie. *Wildlife in the Anthropocene*. Minneapolis: University of Minnesota Press, 2015.

McKibben, Bill. *The End of Nature*. New York: Random House, 1989.

Paquet, Paul C., and Chris T. Darimont. "Wildlife Conservation and Animal Welfare: Two Sides of the Same Coin." *Animal Welfare* 19, no. 2 (2010): 177–90.

Soule, Michael E., and Bruce A. Wilcox. *Conservation Biology: An Evolutionary-Ecological Perspective*. Sunderland, MA: Sinauer, 1980.

Srinivasan, Krithika. "Caring for the Collective: Biopower and Agential Subjectification in Wildlife Conservation." *Environment and Planning D: Society and Space* 32, no. 3 (2014): 501–17.

Van Houtan, Kyle S. "Conservation as Virtue: A Scientific and Social Process for Conservation Ethics." *Conservation Biology* 20, no. 5 (2006): 1367–72.

Wilson, Edward O. "Editorial: On the Future of Conservation Biology." *Conservation Biology* 14, no. 1 (2000): 1–3.

———. *Half-Earth: Our Planet's Fight for Fife*. New York: W. W. Norton, 2016.

CHAPTER ELEVEN

Grieving Salmon and the Politics of Collective Ecological Fieldwork

CLEO WOELFLE-ERSKINE

I learned to grieve rivers by noticing them as dark gaps under the Southern California freeway as I drove through the Santa Ana basin night. In high school, I made this trip once or twice a year, alone in an old Toyota station wagon, driving back to Venice from the San Bernardino Mountains where I learned dry granite headwater streams by bounding from boulder to boulder. Out the window, the dry stream flashed by as dark gaps in the subdivisions. At undercrossings, sand-bottomed washes narrowed between riprap banks, illuminated in orange sodium-lit glow.

What I noticed: dark stillness that hinted at muddy torrents and slow underflow below the dry streambed. I didn't think in hydrologic terms then. I hadn't learned to see alluvial fans under a crust of houses, or notice the geomorphic transition to the flat plain, where over eons floods spread out and filled an ancient canyon with sediment. But I'd read Mike Davis's *Ecology of Fear* and so could imagine flash floods sweeping down, carrying shopping carts, cars, brush, and sometimes people waving their arms for help.[1]

Farther west on the I-10 the city crowded in. Riprap armor at the undercrossings gave way to the Los Angeles River's paved sloping banks. What I imagined: lost braided willow channels and trickling, fishy pools. A vast marsh spreading out, stark green against dun chaparral hills. Curves and meanders hidden by straight, gray concrete flumes. Alone in the dark car, with the radio on, watching the city lights stream by, I longed for this former world.

Noticing became for me a kind of witnessing: of water's flows and ebbs, traces of wandering streams, imagined latent destinies and improbable future renewals. I practiced this witnessing as I came to know other rivers, first as a laborer on a stream restoration crew in New Mexico; next leading kids on explorations of urban Oakland, California, creeks; then as a geology student studying dam removal on Montana's Clark Fork; and, most recently, as an ecologist studying Northern California coastal streams during drought.

In each of these roles I worked with and learned from people who wanted to redress past harms that settlers and their industries had done to the land and water. Each position came with different situated knowledges, field practices, and ethical commitments, but all of my colleagues spoke at some point of being overwhelmed by the scale of harm that had been done. Many became burned out, at least temporarily, by witnessing its effects on other species, on ecohydrological processes, and on cultural relations to the more-than-human world.

For the "we" who are field ecologists, I think the question of how to avoid burnout contains (at least) two questions: How do we not feel the death too much? And what is a better way to not

be burned out by our work? As ecologists, can we study extinction and contamination without shutting down our feelings of
grief and loss, but rather tapping into emotions as a source for
social connection and political action?[2]

To the first question: in my US-based experience, ecologists
are trained to excise mentions of grief at premature death or
suffering from our papers and conference presentations. I think
that many ecologists begin to self-censor expressions of this
grief long before writing, while in the field among colleagues.
Perhaps this is because emotion and affective connection are
framed, sometimes implicitly, during field encounters or methods courses, as unscientific because they are unobjective, a possible source of bias in statistical analysis or interpretation.

The world speaks to field ecologists through data, which
function to distill and recall our encounters with our focal species and its co-inhabitants in the field. The data we collect show
whether an organism lives, dies, grows, reproduces, migrates, or
thrives given certain conditions. We are trained to be curious
about what the data show, whether or not those results match
our expectations or desires. When the data show loss—of a special place; of an individual creature to poisoning, starvation, or
suffocation; or of an entire species to habitat loss or a changing
climate—this can be a good scientific result. "Good science"
because our study design was robust enough to detect a change,
and our models suggested a mechanism for change. If we feel a
thrill in that discovery, in that elegant meshing of theory and
data, then this emotion is totally acceptable to convey in our
conference talks, or even, in a measured way, in research papers.
But feeling the loss of a beloved study species, lamenting and
grieving a stonefly's disappearance from a desert spring, or the
absence of ten thousand rasping monarch butterfly wings from a

steep pine mountain, or a yellow warbler's song in spring? We ecologists rarely share those feelings with our collaborators or in public, and in that repeated silencing, I worry that we lose some capacity to feel, to grieve, and to take action from that grief.

To the second question: queer activist field practices offer one route away from burnout. During the height of the AIDS crisis in the United States, queers and other outcasts turned grief at mounting death of their chosen kin toward public performances of mourning and rage. Works reflecting on this time all convey a sense of collective breathing space that this acting-together-in-the-face-of-extinction created.[3] What was unbearable individual grief became a cathartic, collective rage that spurred political action for medical research, for antidiscrimination legislation, and for social support for people living with AIDS.

In mourning beloved dead in public, the thousands of friends and lovers who came into the streets as ACT UP proclaimed that these dead had lived lives worth grieving. They demanded an end to policies that made HIV-infected bodies killable by neglect and an end to homophobic erasure of the epidemic. These protests, these rituals of grieving and loving, demanded and enacted queer visibility by being together in public. Although I was just a child during the height of the AIDS crisis in the United States, I heard queer and trans elders relive these experiences in the streets later, at vigils for trans people killed by friends, strangers, or the police. I wonder, as I think back on my own encounters with dead and dying study organisms, whether such public mourning for interspecies relations could bring new fire to environmental activism, and perhaps replace affectless terms like "species loss" and "biodiversity" with "death of beloved kin."

In Salmon Creek in central California, where I have spent six field seasons studying juvenile salmon survival through a deepening drought, followed by spectacular floods, I became intensely curious about how and why coho and steelhead chose the pool where they spend their first long, dry summer. In early spring, the young fish can swim freely up- and downstream but then are stuck in whichever place they have chosen once the shallows dry into long, dry stretches of gravel. When salmon disappeared from one week to the next, I looked for raccoon or bird tracks, for any dead bodies, and for clues in the dissolved oxygen readings as to whether they had suffocated or become prey.

Sometimes, when I was alone, I would talk to them and say I was sorry they were starving, were struggling to breathe, were frantic, hiding under leaves from the big, loud mammal. But I didn't rescue them and move them to a different pool, where they might survive. I didn't move them, in part, because other fish already inhabited those deeper pools. Adding fish might mean that none survived. But also, I wanted to know why fish survived in some pools—I wanted to understand processes, causal mechanisms, the dynamic links between flow, habitat, and the species' evolved adaptations to that environment, now changed by drought and human water extraction. I am struck, on writing this, by how when speaking the language of ecology, it's hard to escape industrial and mechanistic language, and hard to think about how to introduce the language of emotions into such statements.

Where early scientists like Charles Darwin and Jean Henri Fabre mixed expressions of wonder and delight into their descriptions of species morphology and behavior, scientific mores no longer permit such diversions.[4] My grief at salmon death took hold of my body, my breath, in the field. Later, numbers on data sheets and in R code back in the lab evoked those feelings again. Yet I didn't even try to write those feelings into my data analysis, even in the more speculative discussion section. This emotional disconnect, however productive for ecological thinking, limits the work that ecology can do in the world, and constrains conservation politics and perhaps ecologists' emotional lives. As humans, can we repress love and grief and fear at extinction without closing off emotional ways of learning and seeing differently? False objectivity constrains our ability to respond. It may also lead us to unquestioningly accept methods and biases handed down from earlier generations.

ON STAYING OPEN TO SUFFERING

My lab-mate Suzanne joins me to recount salmon fry on Salmon Creek during the fall of 2014. The riverine palette is all gold and gray, storm clouds, falling alder leaves, and a strange red-purple opacity to the sulfurous water. The deep pools I swam through in June have shrunk to puddles in long expanses of dry streambed. Suzanne's oxygen probe shows levels around one part per million, in the lethal range for salmon. I switch on a flashlight, crawl toward the edge of the pool, then slither into water barely belly deep. I scan through the murk for a flash of silver. I see just one slowly moving fish through the dim. As we move up the dry streambed to pool after tiny pool, cold seeps through the shredded knees of my wet suit and around my snorkel, bringing decay onto my tongue. I strain for any glimpse of fish. It's not just the low light or the way the redness attenuates my flashlight beam: my heart aches for the hundreds of darting silver bodies I swam through in early summer, for the lives gone missing. In one pool, nine small silver fish flit past. My heart leaps—but then the red pulse of their slow-gasping gills sets up a resonant feeling of suffocation as I struggle to breathe through the snorkel. Here Suzanne measures dissolved oxygen at four parts per million, well below the six parts per million salmon need to thrive. In the next pool, strange purple biofilms bloom up toward the surface; here the oxygen is close to zero, and we find only stickleback.

At one such anoxic pool, Suzanne kneels down and picks up a small dead steelhead in her neoprene-gloved hand. "There must be a lot of morts," she says, using jargon for *mortalities*, or dead fish. "You usually don't see them before the raccoons get to them." The little body is fresh and stiff, their spotted side covered with a whitish film of microbes, their bright eyes glazed over. "So small and skinny," Suzanne says. "They're just losing weight in these small pools." Because of the drought, the stream stopped flowing a month earlier than usual, and it's been months since the fishes' bug prey drifted downstream. Suzanne's response to this single death was not only grief. She seemed, rather, curious and slightly wistful, as if she was seeing the liveliness stilled, a kind of sadness at foreclosed possibilities for smolting, ocean swimming, and a chance at spawning. But alongside that sadness at the individual fish's death, she was fascinated with the relations these deaths-in-drought revealed. Had the young fish who survived sought out wet and oxygenated sanctuary pools? If so, how? Did they smell the groundwater flow? Or did they end up there because other fish chased them out of better, deeper ones?

In my bare hand, the fish is still and not slimy. I know these young fish partly through their jumpiness, their determined flopping when I grab them from a net to weigh and measure them, the pulse of their terror confined in my wet hand. My heart aches at the cold rigidity of the small body, not swimming or flopping or darting under a bank.

Two years later, I join Suzanne to help survey steelhead at her Eel River tributary study site. I'm excited to practice electrofishing, to see this protected stream deep within the University of California Angelo Reserve, and to meet some nice young fish. With a crew of five undergraduates, we pack the forty-pound electrofishing backpack current generator, extra batteries, and assorted buckets, measuring devices, and fish-tagging equipment down a trail, then up a steep, boulder-bed stream thick with lush growth. Water flows quick and clear in the shallow, rocky pools of the headwater stream, and wide and sometimes deep in the larger tributary. One person wears the backpack, trails a metal lead in the water, and passes a long metal wand over the streambed and under the bank. Three or four others follow with dip nets, looking for a white flash when a stunned fish flips on their side, then darting in with the net to scoop them up. While the shocker runs, it beeps and hums. When a fish "flips," they do so for only a second or two. If the netters miss, the shocker shocks again, and everyone hopes someone will net the fish before their heart stops permanently.

We put the netted fish into perforated buckets in the cool stream, then Suzanne and a student work them up: anesthetizing them with Alka-Seltzer; weighing, measuring, and photographing them; scanning them with a microchip reader; and then (if the fish has not previously been caught and tagged) clipping a piece of the tail for genetic analysis, making a small incision on their belly, inserting a rice-sized microchip, and rubbing the incision with a finger to reseal the protective slime. Most start swimming within seconds, flopping in my hand or swimming quickly once placed in the bucket. Over the course of the three days, three or four (of around a hundred) don't recover. These "morts" fall well within the limits of Suzanne's scientific collecting permit. I instinctively count the fish as we approach the pools. They are easily visible in the clear water, though a few turn out to be hiding under the banks. I notice that, especially in very bouldery pools, we capture fewer than I count.

When I mention this to Suzanne, she says she's noticed the same thing. She regrets the deaths and questions the "old guard" logic that shocking doesn't harm the fish or stunt their growth, explaining, "I think we could get better data by snorkeling, estimating length visually, and then fly fishing to get fin clips for genetic analysis." She's planning an extra day of snorkeling, so that she can compare the two methods in her pools and write a paper comparing the two methods. I say it would be an interesting ethics paper, and the undergraduate researcher who's working with us then tells us about her ambivalence toward some of the ways her coresearchers handle organisms they collect: "Sometimes they handle them for fun, or to make a video, not for data. I don't think that's right."

ON THE DIFFERENTIAL SUFFERING OF SALMON AND THEIR CO-INHABITANTS

Like medical doctors, field biologists and ecologists are acculturated during scientific training *not* to feel individual grief, at killing bugs, at letting fish die. This training provides an emotional buffer between scientists who deliberately or accidentally kill or harm animals during the course of their research. Formal ethics trainings in vertebrate research mobilize discourses of humane treatment during handling and killing (that animals not suffer pain and are not killed unnecessarily).

Some field scientists who collect and kill benthic aquatic invertebrates told me that these species do not feel pain (and research seems to back this up).[5] One said, watching mayfly, stonefly, caddisfly, and fly larvae squirm as he poured ethanol over them, that he felt bad when he killed them, that he thought they were struggling to escape and live, even if they lacked pain receptors or memory pathways.

Scientists who work with stream fishes sometimes use observation (either directly or with cameras) but often also capture, handle, weigh, measure, and tag fishes by implanting microchips, clipping fins, or injecting a colored dye into the skin. Most scientists I've talked to feel that plants, algae, water, and minerals are not sentient and thus are exempt from ethical consideration on the level of the individual, although wantonly destructing populations of plants is unethical. Fish biologists have shared different views on stunning fish with electroshockers versus catching them in nets or with a rod and reel. Some feel strongly that electrofishing kills fewer fish, while others feel that net seining causes less damage and death. Standard practice for anesthetizing salmonids during handling and surgery is via carbon dioxide (produced by Alka-Seltzer tablets dropped in their water bucket), to reduce tissue damage from flopping. This method replaced an earlier anesthetic that caused more accidental deaths.

Does this training enhance or diminish our capacity to grieve for populations and species under threat of extinction? In my own case, I think the training in observation, and the process of reckoning with the ethics of different kinds of death, enhances that capacity to grieve, but I'm still struggling to find an outlet for that grief— a way for that grief to work for making different relations with more-than-human kin, and against unremarked death that makes other species killable in the wake of settler resource extraction logics. But then norms of "objective" writing and imposing emotional distance in discussing our work frustrate my attempts to reckon with that grief, and to make a queer ecological politics of mourning dead kin, and to bring all of myself to my scientific work.

In 2017, I took my own graduate students into the field with me for the first time. As we're preparing for the trip, I tell them that I study fishes who are on the brink of extinction, that individual fish face starvation or suffocation or being washed away before they've even emerged from the egg. As I teach them how to do snorkel counts and measure dissolved oxygen in the field, I listen for my students' expressions of sadness and respond with my own feelings at witnessing fishes' ongoing struggles for survival and my ethical opposition to using scientific methods that might subject them to further harm. Then, once we're in the field, I adapt the best I can to contingencies and surprises that storms or drought have thrown up: sensors buried in gravel, trees dropped across study pools, high temperatures that make salmon more likely to die if handled. I don't know if these ethical conversations save any fish lives, or affect my students' emotional lives. But when I've shared this writing on grief in the field with colleagues, many have responded with their own stories of unexpressed grief (or joy or anger) at witnessing beloved species' death or distress, and in that space of exchange and recognition, we find some solidarity to continue with the neverending work of caring in and for the world.

NOTES

1. Mike Davis, *Ecology of Fear: Los Angeles and the Imagination of Disaster* (New York: Vintage, 1999).

2. Or field biologists, or ecohydrologists, or ecogeomorphologists: I include here anyone who studies the interplay of species and elementals in the field.

3. I'm thinking here of David Wojnarowicz, *Close to the Knives: A Memoir of Disintegration* (New York: Vintage, 1991); Eve Sedgwick, "White Glasses," in *Tendencies* (Durham, NC: Duke University Press, 1993); Leo Bersani, "Is the Rectum a Grave," *October* 43 (Winter 1987): 197–222; Deborah Gould, *Moving Politics: Emotion and ACT UP's Fight against AIDS* (Chicago: Chicago University Press, 2009), among others.

4. This sense of wonder pervades most of Darwin's writing, and Jean Henri Fabre's *Fabre's Book of Insects* (Mineola, NY: Dover, 1998).

5. Since larval benthic (stream-bottom) invertebrates are widespread and abundant, and because identification measures require preservation and dissection, practices of killing/preserving in ethanol are nearly universal among researchers.

BIBLIOGRAPHY

Bersani, Leo. "Is the Rectum a Grave?" *October* 43 (Winter 1987): 197–222.

Davis, Mike. *Ecology of Fear: Los Angeles and the Imagination of Disaster.* New York: Vintage, 1999.

Fabre, Jean Henri. *Fabre's Book of Insects.* Mineola, NY: Dover, 1998.

Gould, Deborah B. *Moving Politics: Emotion and ACT UP's Fight against AIDS.* Chicago: University of Chicago Press, 2009.

Sedgwick, Eve Kosofsky. "White Glasses." In *Tendencies*, 252–66. Durham, NC: Duke University Press, 1993.

Wojnarowicz, David. *Close to the Knives: A Memoir of Disintegration.* New York: Vintage, 1991.

CHAPTER TWELVE

Witnessing Grief

Feminist Perspectives on the Loss-Body-Mind-Self-Other Nexus and Permission to Express Feelings

AVRIL MADDRELL AND ELIZABETH OLSON

THE CONTENTS OF MY PURSE

Elizabeth Olson

earring

EpiPen

broken pen

working pen

potato chip

hair clip

sock

lipstick

pretzel stick

box of mints

(not gluten free)

my dad's phone
(he died recently)
painkillers
dirt
dead-weight.

EMPTY

Avril Maddrell

Empty belly,
Full breasts;
Empty arms,
Full of grief.

EMBODIED AND INTIMATE
AUTOBIOGRAPHICAL ACCOUNTS

These two autobiographical poems, written on different continents, span some sixteen years; they speak for themselves (and those they enfold), but they also speak to each other. Both speak of poetic response to death and loss—literally and metaphorically. They also highlight the intermeshed materiality and embodiment of grief, the sheer viscerality and emotional weight of grief at that time; grief at once immaterial and physical burden. Our reasons for writing this chapter together were driven by mutual respect for each other's work, and enough stolen conversations at conferences to suspect that the sum of our parts might amount to a worthwhile whole. We didn't know that we had both written poems in and about our experiences of grief until we started the writing process.

We wrote the poems at times of acute unanticipated bereavement: one in response to the death of a parent, a generation above, and one for a child, the next generation, stillborn. We draw on these separate, deeply intimate life-spaces and expressions as an entry point to explore understandings of witnessing grief and grieving in ourselves and others, notably feminist perspectives on the intersecting body-mind-self-other nexus. It is a response to calls in feminist scholarship to "write ourselves into the analysis."[1] We draw on our own experience not to privilege it—death is part of the natural life cycle, and there are many communities in which premature death is a daily reality—rather, we acknowledge the situatedness of our understanding in our personal experience in order to reflect on the meaning and politics of death, bereavement, and witnessing grief.[2] Like others in this collection, we argue that autobiography and intimate geographies offer insight and meaningful ways of understanding the world and are therefore significant for reflecting on the politics of knowledge production (that is, what knowledge and whose knowledge is deemed valid) as well as the nature and adequacy of public services (in this case those such as health care and bereavement support).[3]

EMPTINESS, WEIGHT, AND PERMISSION

Intimate writing can be methodologically "muddy" and raise a number of ethical questions.[4] Permission and consent were issues both of us struggled with in writing this piece because, while autobiographical, our experiences were not in isolation; they were experienced in relation to and with others—not least the deceased. We each wrestled with what we could/should say in relation to the dead and the living. But questions of permission go beyond these personal and ethical considerations; they also speak to the framing and politics of permission to grieve and express that grief in social contexts. One such context is that of our profession.

AVRIL

Including "Empty" in this piece prompted me to reflect on a number of issues and vulnerabilities, including what I could/ should say about my most vulnerable self in a professional context. When our second child was stillborn at term in May 1998, I used private writing as a means to express my love, my loss, and the negotiation of our ongoing family life. It was to these writings, added to periodically over the years, that I turned when Betsy and I began collaborating on this piece. While I have spoken and written extensively on geographies of death and remembrance in the context of feminist emotional-affective cultural geographies for more than ten years, always acknowledging that this is grounded in my own experience of bereavement, this work has focused on establishing a conceptual framework and analyzing the practices, experiences, and expressions of others. It is one thing to draw on one's own experience; it is another to lay it bare. Over the years I have shared my experience in public arenas, such as bereavement support networks or health care practitioner trainings, but writing here makes different demands, has different implications. It is a matter of being prepared to give permission to myself to write about my own most deep and personal experience and being prepared to make my most vulnerable self public within my professional context. Undoubtedly, the growing body of work on the emotional-affective geographies of death, loss, and remembrance as well as those on intimacy and autobiography provide a context and rationale for deeply personal reflections such as this. Nonetheless, it may be deemed professionally risky by some, but it is important for several reasons. First, as discussed earlier, studying intimacy and embodiment is important and should be accepted and respected as a valid form of knowledge; second, effective scholarship on geographies of death needs to be attentive and sensitive to the realities of the lived experience of death and bereavement. Consequently, I consider this risk worthwhile, necessary even. But what to share and in what form?

Writing this chapter raised questions about how much to say and on whose behalf. What did I have permission to say about others? I considered using a letter I wrote but was uncomfortable with this because it had been written to another, prompting me to focus on something centered squarely on my own experience. "Empty" is a call-and-response verse that serves as a witness account of my own emotional-embodied experience of acute loss: the interweaving of physiological responses to giving birth but having no baby to hold, nor to feed, and my bereavement as a mother, are recorded in the simultaneous, interactive, and compounding emptiness-fullness, which is expressed through naming my disenfranchised body parts.

My writings record the ongoing journey of living with loss, carrying on, including the periodic ebb and flow of the experience of emptiness and fullness in subsequent years; they also speak of *weight*. An anniversary of this bereavement *"came with a thud. I felt heavy, pregnant with grief, felt weighted, that emotional paralysis which requires the dragging manipulation of one leg, then the other."* Notions of weight run through Betsy's poem "The contents of my purse," which prompts reflection on how rules of permission are held close or violated in periods of intense grief, and the discussion that follows links this to a commentary on the gendered and racialized norms of expression in public places.

BETSY

"The contents of my purse" was an attempt to expose the problem of permission in grief. As I went through the motions of trying to help my mother discard my father's possessions, my purse became literally heavier and cluttered with the remnants of our three weeks in a cardiac intensive care unit. I still had a bottle of ibuprofen to counteract back and shoulder pain from hours spent bent over his bed to prevent him from interfering with equipment. This was jammed beside less trivial objects such as my son's EpiPen, and more trivial ones such as mints purchased without first checking for gluten (because who can think about checking labels during times like these). My grief became unexpectedly manifest in my purse, itself simultaneously obtrusive and concealing, something that I could even disregard when the weight was forgotten in brief moments when I achieved a state of distraction and security.

I opened my purse in a mobile phone store where I went to find out what to do with my father's phone, this thing that was both inert and triggering, both weight and memory. I felt my heart rate rise even as the muscle itself seemed to find a way to dig deeper back into my chest. I didn't know whether to cry or throw something, and I briefly considered wildly rampaging through the crowded shop, hurling the contents of my purse for all to see, exposing myself to the point where permission is no longer required because I had already moved far beyond the expectations for that place. I wanted to violate the rules of conduct that required my careful concealment. Putting death, darkness, and derailment in the styling of a children's poem offends expectations and mimics the ways that places become disrupted in and through grief. I was unwilling to violate the norms of permission in the phone store, but I wanted to break something with the weight I felt at that time. "The contents of my purse" did this for me.

Already, the standard rules of permission and how we interfaced with them had been turned kaleidoscopic during my father's illness and death. Mom was angry with the Catholic chaplain. My sister and I didn't ask anyone to approve our new intimacy with our father's body required to keep him safe, calm, and comfortable. And after allowing the grief to settle in us in the private rooms reserved for loved ones immediately after death, my mom, sister, and I walked through the lobby of the ICU laughing loudly, disruptively, with all the tears and pain and humor that these singular moments evoke. Inappropriate laughter in the wrong place and wrong time runs in my family, passed securely from generation to generation, exemplified at this time by unsuccessfully muffled guffaws in church and the recognizable holding in of explosive laughter in quiet meetings and serious discussions. In moments of intense grief, we easily disregarded permissions intended to maintain public order, didn't bother seeking permissions, and seemed to be forgiven or overlooked for our disruptions. It could be that intense grief denies permission its place, sometimes through the designation of a material space where permission is not required, and other times through excuses for the grieving. It was our ticket to unquestioned, unfettered public emoting, at least in those few places where grief is standard and expected.

PERMISSION TO EMOTE? THE RISKS OF EMOTIONS OUT OF PLACE

It is here, at the point of drawing our stories together and at the interface of space and normativity, that the uneven politics of permission in grief are exposed and where they become instructive beyond the personal. Emoting improperly in place is widely recognized as gendered.[5] Throughout history, women's public emotions have been cast as disproportionately subject to external influences such as witchcraft and the internal dynamics of reproductive organs, with hysteria being perhaps the most popular diagnosis for women's public emotions perceived to be out of the ordinary.[6] Deeming someone "hysterical" has had a surge in popularity with the recent rise of authoritarianism, such that political pundits freely use the word to describe women, from protesters on the streets to US senators, when aiming to discredit their views.[7]

If we also pay attention to when permission for emotion is granted or denied, we notice the symbolic maneuvers of these moments: (1) women ignore norms of permission in the streets and in the statehouses, and (2) authoritarians or their supporters try to supplant and devalue the political act with descriptors of out-of-place emotion. Attempts to denigrate or repress those who violate norms of permission are not only gendered but reflective of race, class, and citizenship that are characteristic of the constitution of difference in public space.[8] Cases like that of Sandra Bland, an African American woman whose justifiable anger at her treatment during an unnecessary traffic stop caused her death, are reminders that even legitimate public challenging of the normative order of permission is dangerous when expressed by certain bodies. The denial of a need to seek permission can be even more powerful (as well as potentially more dangerous) in the racialized and classed female body, as illustrated by the revolt by female detainees in the UK Yarl's Wood detention center as they exposed their breasts and genitals in protest of their dehumanization, with the knowledge that such a move might draw the attention of the media.[9] Not asking permission for public emotions can be an intentional or unintentional move toward challenging the normative order of space, and it can also be dangerous in its radical insistence for space.

CONCLUDING THOUGHTS

The significance of the body as a geographic space and text, as well as a site of embodied experience and meaning-making, has become rooted in geographic scholarship over the last two decades.[10] This includes the pregnant body; the weight-losing body; the body as a site of experience, knowledge, emotion, and affect, but also of identity, power, and political expression. Furthermore, the body-mind is meshed with significant material and virtual spaces in dynamic emotional maps of loss and consolation.[11] However, while individual embodied accounts can be rich, the focus on bodies does not necessitate an atomistic, individualist approach; embodied experience is also relational, often, at least in part, shared.

We hope that these short reflections illustrate the ways in which individual experiences can speak on their own behalf and to each other. We also hope this piece might encourage others to give themselves permission to explore their autobiographical experience of loss, of whatever form, and that within the academy such writings are recognized as capable of providing valuable scholarly insights to our collective understanding. Furthermore, we hope that these reflections will also prompt wider critical reflections on the politics of who has permission to express themselves, including their grief and other emotions deemed socially, spatially, and temporally "inappropriate," without prejudice.

ACKNOWLEDGMENTS

The authors would like to thank the Maddrell Mander family and the Olson Baruch family.

NOTES

1. Jane F. Gilgun and Laura McLeod, "Gendering Violence," *Studies in Symbolic Interactionism* 22 (1999): 167–93.

2. Olivia Stevenson, Charlotte Kenten, and Avril Maddrell, "Editorial: And Now the End Is Near: Enlivening and Politicising the Geographies of Dying, Death and Mourning," *Social and Cultural Geography* 17, no. 2 (2016): 153–65; Kathryn Gillespie "Witnessing Animal Others: Bearing Witness, Grief, and the Political Function of Emotion," *Hypatia* 31, no. 3 (2016): 572–88.

3. See Pamela Moss, ed., *Placing Autobiography in Geography* (Syracuse, NY: Syracuse University Press, 2001); Pamela Moss and Courtney Donovan, "Introduction," in *Writing Intimacy into Feminist Geography*, ed. Pamela Moss and Courtney Donovan (London: Routledge, 2017), 3–30.

4. Moss and Donovan, "Introduction."

5. Avril Maddrell, "Living with the Deceased: Absence, Presence and Absence-Presence," *Cultural Geographies* 20, no. 4 (2013): 501–22.

6. Cecilia Tasca, Mariangela Rapetti, Mauro Giovanni Carta, and Bianca Fadda, "Women and Hysteria in the History of Mental Health," *Clinical Practice and Epidemiology in Mental Health* 8, no. 1 (2012): 110–19.

7. "Good Morning Britain" interview by Piers Morgan, January 31, 2017, video, 2:32, featuring Owen Jones, https://www.theguardian.com/us-news/video/2017/jan/31/owen-jones-and-piers-morgan-clash-over-anti-trump-protests-video; Leinz Valens, "Columnist Kirsten Powers: 'How Was Sen. Harris Hysterical?,'" CNN Politics, June 14, 2014, www.cnn.com/2017/06/13/politics/powers-miller-kamala-harris-hysterical-sessions-hearing-ac360-cnntv/index.html.

8. Susan Ruddick, "Constructing Difference in Public Spaces: Race, Class, and Gender as Interlocking Systems," *Urban Geography* 17, no. 2 (1996): 132–51.

9. Imogen Tyler, "Naked Protest: The Maternal Politics of Citizenship and Revolt," *Citizenship Studies* 17, no. 2 (2013): 211–26.

10. See, for example, Bronwyn Davies, Jenny Browne, Susanne Gannon, Eileen Honan, and Margaret Somerville, "Embodied Women at Work in Neoliberal Times and Places," *Gender, Work and Organization* 12, no. 4 (2005): 343–62; Robyn Longhurst, "The Body," in

Cultural Geography: A Critical Dictionary of Key Concepts, ed. David Atkinson, Peter Jackson, David Sibley, and Neil Washbourne (London: I. B. Tauris, 2005), 91–96.

11. Avril Maddrell, "Mapping Grief: A Conceptual Framework for Understanding the Spatialities of Bereavement, Mourning and Remembrance," *Social and Cultural Geography* 17, no. 2 (2016): 166–88.

BIBLIOGRAPHY

Davies, Bronwyn, Jenny Browne, Susanne Gannon, Eileen Honan, and Margaret Somerville. "Embodied Women at Work in Neoliberal Times and Places." *Gender, Work and Organization* 12, no. 4 (2005): 343–62.

Gilgun, Jane F., and Laura McLeod. "Gendering Violence." *Studies in Symbolic Interactionism* 22 (1999): 167–93.

Gillespie, Kathryn. "Witnessing Animal Others: Bearing Witness, Grief, and the Political Function of Emotion." *Hypatia* 31, no. 3 (2016): 572–88.

Longhurst, Robyn. "The Body." In *Cultural Geography. A Critical Dictionary of Key Concepts*, edited by David Atkinson, Peter Jackson, David Sibley, and Neil Washbourne, 91–96. London: I. B. Tauris, 2005.

Maddrell, Avril. "Living with the Deceased: Absence, Presence and Absence-Presence." *Cultural Geographies* 20, no. 4 (2013): 501–22

———. "Mapping Grief: A Conceptual Framework for Understanding the Spatialities of Bereavement, Mourning and Remembrance." *Social and Cultural Geography* 17, no. 2 (2016): 166–88.

Moss, Pamela, ed. *Placing Autobiography in Geography*. Syracuse, NY: Syracuse University Press, 2001.

Moss, Pamela, and Courtney Donovan, eds. "Introduction." In *Writing Intimacy into Feminist Geography*, edited by Pamela Moss and Courtney Donovan, 3–30. London: Routledge, 2017.

Ruddick, Susan. "Constructing Difference in Public Spaces: Race, Class, and Gender as Interlocking Systems." *Urban Geography* 17, no. 2 (1996): 132–51.

Stevenson, Olivia, Charlotte Kenten, and Avril Maddrell. "Editorial: And Now the End Is Near: Enlivening and Politicising the Geographies of Dying, Death and Mourning." *Social and Cultural Geography* 17, no. 1 (2016): 153–65.

Tasca, Cecilia, Mariangela Rapetti, Mauro Giovanni Carta, and Bianca Fadda. "Women and Hysteria in the History of Mental Health." *Clinical Practice and Epidemiology in Mental Health* 8, no. 1 (2012): 110–19.

Tyler, Imogen. "Naked Protest: The Maternal Politics of Citizenship and Revolt." *Citizenship Studies* 17, no. 2 (2013): 211–26.

CHAPTER THIRTEEN

Self-Care and Trauma

Locating the Time and Space to Grieve

DANA CUOMO

> grieve. so that you can be free to feel something else.
> —Nayyirah Waheed

I accepted the invitation to contribute a chapter for this book project and immediately regretted the decision. My reluctance stemmed not from overcommitment; I had the time. Nor from lack of material; I study domestic violence. Nor from uncertainty about the importance of this project; our panel discussions at the 2015 annual meeting of the American Association of Geographers made clear the need and desire for sustained engagement on the topic. Rather, I felt exhausted thinking about how to summon the emotional energy to write about grief, trauma, and violence.

Much had changed in the two years between the panel discussions and sitting down to write this chapter. I finished my doctorate and transitioned into a job at the University of Washington providing advocacy services for survivors of interpersonal violence. Working as a victim advocate has afforded me financial stability, health insurance, and time to apply for tenure-track positions in a competitive academic job market. Working as a victim advocate has also left me experiencing periods of secondary trauma and burnout. I held a similar position before graduate school, knew the emotional toll associated with daily exposure to trauma, and entered the job with a conscious plan for self-care. However, what I failed to anticipate were the emotional effects of working full-time as a victim advocate while applying for academic jobs and churning out publications centered on domestic violence. I regularly woke up early to write in the dark hours of the morning before arriving at the office, where I spent the day providing advocacy services to survivors of sexual assault and relationship violence. Between writing and direct service, I was enveloped in constant exposure to trauma and violence. Predictably, the schedule became unsustainable and unhealthy. Unhealthy not only because I sensed the onset of burnout but also because I lacked the space and time to process—to grieve—the pain and trauma that I was witnessing in my academic writing and professional work.

In what follows, I draw on my fluid identity as a domestic violence scholar and victim advocate to reflect on the self-care practices that I employ—sometimes unsuccessfully—to prevent secondary trauma. For scholars who study violence, but who remain embedded within that trauma, permitting oneself to grieve creates a host of challenges. Where do we process grief when we lack distance from the trauma? How do we process grief when we feel vulnerable or burned out? What emotional spaces help support healthy grieving? How do we create distance from violence to grieve what we have witnessed? With recognition of my own experiences of secondary trauma and in the spirit of hope and healing, I detail the practices that I utilize in my research, writing, and professional work to reflect on the role of time and space in the grieving process.

EVERYDAY TRAUMA

As an expert in trauma exposure, Laura van Dernoot Lipsky encourages those of us who witness trauma to actively acknowledge the impacts of this witnessing in order to remain effective in our work over time.[1] She argues that remaining emotionally present not only sustains us as individuals but also reduces the likelihood that we do harm to those around us. Witnessing violence, pain, and suffering while engaged in academic fieldwork is difficult. Yet the field is only one of many sites in which we encounter trauma. What we read before falling asleep, the images we consume on television, the end-of-life care we provide to an ill family member or companion animal, the latest ecological disaster or humanitarian crisis all take a cumulative toll. For those of us exposed to violence and trauma in the field, it can easily follow us home and spill into the trauma already present in our everyday lives. Van Dernoot Lipsky also emphasizes that the effects of individual witnessing are unequal, particularly as we situate daily trauma and violence within broader systems of oppression. The degree to which trauma affects us individually alters and intensifies when we consider institutional and systemic oppressions like racism, (hetero)sexism, xenophobia, ableism, and classism.

Despite our differences as individuals, those of us exposed to ongoing trauma experience shared responses in how we cope, ranging from feelings of guilt to hypervigilance to cynicism to chronic exhaustion.[2] My red flag for the onset of secondary trauma is when I begin to feel numb and lack the ability to empathize with those around me. When I reflect on how numbing manifests slowly over time, I notice myself less troubled by the sheer volume of sexual assault and relationship violence occurring in the world. Or, when I begin to compare stories of interpersonal violence and rank those stories on a continuum of less to more severe. Or, when I manage to have just enough empathetic capacity to work one-on-one with my clients during the day, but I go home at night and roll my eyes when my partner complains about his colleagues. Intellectually, I recognize how trauma exposure affects me negatively and in turn reduces my capacity to care for others. Practically, integrating a successful plan of self-care into my daily life to combat trauma exposure remains an ongoing journey. I have found utility in the concepts of time and space as a means to help me feel present. More specifically, my self-care practice centers on locating the hidden moments of time and space to consciously make room for processing grief, reducing my exposure to trauma, and remaining emotionally engaged in my everyday, activist and academic life.

RECLAIMING (MY) TIME

A successful self-care practice for witnessing daily trauma and violence does not require a month away from work without internet, sipping chilled wine under an umbrella while staring aimlessly at the ocean. Although that kind of escape also serves a purpose, it reinforces the notion that self-care happens as an addendum to our daily lives and only after we have reached our breaking point. As a staff employee on a twelve-month contract and with a finite number of vacation days, I have learned to make small adjustments in how I manage my daily schedule to process the trauma and violence that I witness.

Barring special or emergent circumstances, I have reduced all my meetings with student-survivors by five minutes, an amount of time that hardly seems worth the effort yet opens up numerous opportunities for self-care. In the field of victim advocacy, caseloads are always high. On college campuses, as universities dedicate more resources to prevention training, not only have students become more adept at accurately recognizing the dynamics of an unhealthy relationship or identifying nonconsensual sex as sexual assault, but survivors are also actively accessing advocacy services in higher numbers. Following campus interpersonal violence trainings, I see a bump in requests for meetings in the subsequent weeks. Unfortunately, the more frequent requests for advocacy services have not been matched by increased staffing. This, in turn, places increased pressure on advocates to fit more survivors into the workday, leading to greater risk for secondary trauma. Reducing by a fraction the amount of time I spend with each student allows me to build in more regular self-care throughout the day. I utilize the extra five minutes differently depending on what I sense my mind, heart, and body need. If hours have passed since I last left the office, I take a quick walk around the building to stretch my legs. After intense meetings, I shut my door, close my eyes, and slow my breathing until I feel my heart rate relax. When a colleague is available, I might share a student's story as a means to express my own feelings of sadness or outrage. Sometimes I watch puppy videos on YouTube.

Reclaiming small amounts of time for self-care in my work as a victim advocate takes deliberate effort. The same is true for research in academia, where the long-term effects of trauma exposure might not appear as evident when fieldwork is temporary or located far away. I have written about the boundary-making strategies that I utilize in the field to protect my emotional health while conducting research on violence.[3] Yet, as academics, trauma exposure follows us from the field back to the academy and occurs all the time, including in our relationships with colleagues or when advising students. Reclaiming time can include small shifts in the length of meetings with students, or in reserving time for a walk before or after office hours. Reclaiming time for self-care within academia also means establishing boundaries with students and acknowledging when to hand over a student's trauma to someone better equipped.

Feminist scholars engage in many unacknowledged forms of service within our departments. When we bring our research into the classroom and speak directly about violence, students often identify us as trusted allies and disclose experiences of interpersonal violence. Survivor disclosures occur in writing assignments, in classroom discussion, and in private conversations during office hours. These disclosures might detail recent experiences of violence that require immediate medical care and safety planning, or childhood abuse suffered long ago. I always feel gratitude when students disclose experiences of interpersonal violence to me. I understand student disclosures as confirmation that I have discussed interpersonal violence in a way that validates their own experiences. I listen intently and affirm the courage it takes to share what they did. I make clear that what happened was not their fault, and I explain that I would like to connect them to support services on campus. In urgent situations, I offer to walk the student to the advocate's office for an introduction and gentle handoff.

Referring student-survivors of trauma to support services is an act of self-care. When I arrive at a new institution, I invite the campus advocate to coffee in anticipation that our paths will cross before long. Some institutions dedicate stand-alone advocates for survivors of interpersonal violence, while other institutions fold advocacy services into on-campus counseling, or contract with local, community-based domestic violence and rape crisis centers. I ask how to refer a student and if the advocate takes walk-in appointments. I inquire about the campus reporting process and if the advocate accompanies students to court or police interviews. I enter the advocate's number into my phone. My preemptive meeting with the campus advocate results in valuable information about resources and allows me to confidently tell a student that I am referring them to someone I trust.

Clarifying my role with students allows me to reclaim time in my everyday life to remain emotionally present. By referring a student to campus resources, I remain connected to the student's well-being, while reducing my own exposure to trauma. As an instructor, I willingly provide informal accommodations to help student-survivors remain academically engaged in my classroom. However, as an instructor, it is not my role to safety plan, discuss reporting options, accompany a student to court, or communicate with other professors about a student's academic needs. By referring students to already-existing campus resources, I establish clear boundaries and role expectations, while also reclaiming time for my self-care practice without taking on new trauma that does not belong to me.

DEDICATING SPACE

Locating emotional space to create distance from trauma and to support healthy grieving remains an ongoing endeavor in my self-care practice. In creating space to process grief, I have identified the spaces that I want to protect from trauma exposure.

My home is one such space. As a victim advocate, leaving the stories of violence and trauma at the office represents a critical component for longevity in the profession. Communication between survivors and victim advocates is protected by confidentiality, a legal privilege similar to a doctor-patient relationship. Even if I wanted to process the violence and trauma that I hear on a daily basis with my family and friends, confidentiality restricts where and with whom I can share such stories. Consequently, the threshold of my home represents a literal and conceptual boundary for where processing the grief associated with trauma starts and stops.

I rely on the space between my home and office to remain emotionally present and to actively grieve all that I witness throughout the day. I currently live five miles from work and commute by bike. I share a car with my partner, and what began as a practical solution to a limited resource has turned into a critical component of my self-care practice. I conceptualize my five-mile commute as a distinct space and extended boundary that connects me to my office and home. Although commuting is the one consistent and predictable aspect of my day, the morning and evening rides serve different purposes in my self-care practice.

I utilize the morning commute to center myself for the day. As I begin riding, I envision my schedule and how I might carve out time to work on outstanding projects. My heart rate remains slow in the morning, and I deliberately ease into a conscious awareness of my surroundings. The winding Burke-Gilman Trail marks the majority of my commute, extending along multiple bodies of water in Seattle. I notice the birds splashing, I appreciate the technique of the kayakers and rowers, and I imagine living in one of the coveted houseboats along the lake's edge.

I acknowledge the other daily commuters with a nod of my head, as I stay focused on the path forward. When the sky is clear, I see Mount Rainier in the distance. The volcano embodies a commanding presence in the landscape and offers perspective that helps me feel grounded. I ride hard enough to stay warm through the chilly mornings, but stop short of overextending myself or breaking a sweat. My morning commute to work is its own space that I use to ready myself for the day, and I arrive calm and present.

The commute home serves an entirely different purpose. Before I leave the office, I write down everything that I ran out of time to accomplish. With an ever-increasing caseload, I always fear forgetting a task that I promised a student-survivor. After feeling fairly assured that I have a comprehensive list to start the next day, I leave the office and meander through the side streets to the trail that leads me home. It is here that I begin to ride intensely. Even though I am mentally fatigued, I work to increase my heart rate until my legs begin to burn. I feel frazzled at the start of the ride. My mind races, jumping from one thought to the next, but I intentionally work to redirect my focus on remaining present. I feel the weather on my face—wind, rain, or sunshine depending on the season—as I let go of each story that I listened to throughout the day. I inhale with deep, long breaths. I exhale forcefully, audibly, fully releasing the air from my lungs. Before long, my mind stops spinning and I feel more grounded. As I ride the secondary trauma out of my body, I arrive home physically tired but mentally alert. Of course, worries or concerns about a student-survivor occasionally enter my mind as I zone out to the television in the evening or while falling asleep. However, I can usually catch those worries creeping into my consciousness, put them on pause, and know that tomorrow offers another day to reengage with the work.

My self-care practice, while I work as a victim advocate with daily exposure to trauma and violence, has evolved into a more deliberate exercise than when I last conducted academic field-work. Yet the strategies for creating distance and bounding exposure to trauma and violence to certain spaces are applicable regardless of where along the continuum of advocate and scholar I fall. As my self-care practice has evolved, one constant space that remains dedicated to grieving the trauma that I witness regardless of my scholar-advocate identity is my therapist's office. Perhaps self-explanatory and obvious, the opportunity to have a dedicated space to feel the range of emotions that accompany exposure to violence and trauma with professional support cannot be understated. In dedicating space for where I permit trauma exposure to occur and learning how to restrict trauma exposure from entering the spaces I wish to protect, I find myself better equipped to grieve the violence and trauma that I witness.

PRACTICING SELF-CARE

Grieving requires space and time to process the violence and trauma witnessed. Part of my self-care practice is dedicated to finding the hidden moments of time and space throughout the day to consciously and consistently make room to grieve. Another piece of my self-care practice concerns reducing exposure to trauma and violence. In my academic life, reducing exposure to trauma and violence means I might deliberately choose to avoid engaging with the empirical data from my research. This chapter offers one such example. I love to write, and I find the exercise of writing therapeutic. Yet when immersed in trauma and violence as a victim advocate, writing about the trauma and violence encountered in my fieldwork becomes an exhausting and anxiety-inducing endeavor. There are also some empirical accounts from my research that I will never share through writing; it is simply too painful, depressing, and retraumatizing to reimmerse myself in those moments. Instead, for the last two years, I have sought other ways to contribute to academic conversations, whether writing about methodology, editing themed journal issues, or detailing the self-care strategies that I utilize as a scholar-activist.

In identifying when I have reached capacity for engaging in the stories of trauma that I encounter in my academic and advocate life, I establish boundaries. These boundaries include where I process grief, when I encounter trauma, and even what occupies the focus of my writing. Often, the most challenging part of establishing boundaries is holding myself to them. To conduct ethnographic, empirical accounts of trauma and violence over time requires an ongoing and proactive self-care practice. My self-care practice continues to evolve, and through its evolution, I better position myself to continue research that leads me to witness trauma and violence, while remaining healthy and emotionally present.

NOTES

1. Laura van Dernoot Lipsky, *Trauma Stewardship: An Everyday Guide to Caring for Self While Caring for Others* (San Francisco: Berrett-Koehler, 2009).

2. van Dernoot Lipsky, *Trauma Stewardship*.

3. Dana Cuomo and Vanessa A. Massaro, "Boundary-Making in Feminist Research: New Methodologies for 'Intimate Insiders,'" *Gender, Place and Culture*. 23, no. 1 (2016): 94–106.

BIBLIOGRAPHY

Cuomo, Dana, and Massaro, Vanessa A. "Boundary-Making in Feminist Research: New Methodologies for 'Intimate Insiders.'" *Gender, Place and Culture.* 23, no. 1 (2016): 94–106.

van Dernoot Lipsky, Laura. *Trauma Stewardship: An Everyday Guide to Caring for Self While Caring for Others.* San Francisco: Berrett-Koehler, 2009.

EPILOGUE

PATRICIA J. LOPEZ AND KATHRYN
GILLESPIE

What are the words you do not yet have? What do
you need to say? What are the tyrannies you swallow
day by day and attempt to make your own, until you
will sicken and die of them, still in silence?

> —Audre Lorde, "The Transformation of Silence
> into Action"

As we ruminate on the sharing of these stories of grief, we return
to one of our guiding questions: Why grief? What is it about
grief (as opposed to anger, sadness, or simply "emotions" more
broadly) that requires its own theories and stories? What power
and potency does grief possess in its feeling and sharing?

Grief and the act of grieving are transformative; we move
through grief, emerging as someone different, changed, altered
in unfamiliar ways by the affective rupture that took hold of us.
This transformation can be a site for acknowledging interpersonal connection, relationality, friendship, and care. Grief is
also a particular manifestation of love—an acknowledgment
and heart-centered expression of what and who we care deeply
about. Far from being only a private or interpersonal emotion,

though, love—and love articulated as grief—is a radical form of resistance, especially in spaces where grief, love, and emotion are out of place, and especially in loving, caring for, and grieving those whom we are taught not to grieve. This collection, then, has aimed to create an opening for this feeling and expression to occur in a way that can be shared with and by others—to break some of the silence surrounding the many ways grief manifests in our lives and work and to reframe how we think about, theorize, feel, and respond to grief.

Grief, as we have already mentioned in the introduction, is an emotion that is singular and insular except when it is collective for public tragedies.[1] Public expression of personal grief is emotion out-of-place, or "disenfranchised grief... that is experienced when a loss cannot be openly acknowledged, socially sanctioned, or publicly mourned," and is further mediated through scales and hierarchies of grief.[2] Grief is often socially disciplined, as many of the authors have illustrated. Ritual burial, temporal bereavement, and performative emotionality are all frames through which grief is tidily packaged for public consumption and experience. Emotions out-of-place make others feel uncomfortable; *grief* out-of-place or outside the boundaries of prescribed acceptable time frames, methods, and spaces for grieving disrupts normative ideas about emotion, relationality, and the varied natures of loss.

Grief is a profoundly transformative emotion. As the authors have highlighted throughout these chapters, the experience of grieving—the deep embodied affective ruptures that occur as a result—change people fundamentally. Grief is written into the body, on communities of bodies—transforming them indelibly.[3] Writing about grief, in these moments, is not necessarily healing, for the wounds that we carry are deeply woven into the fabric of who we are in ways that may require much more time, care, support, and processing than sharing in this context allows. Still, the authors who have shared their pain and vulnerability here have been incredibly generous not only in sharing the ways they themselves have been transformed by grief but also in demonstrating how sharing this grief with others enacts the very transformation we hope to prompt with this collection—a transformation of the structures in which we live, work, and grieve, and their receptiveness to these truths being spoken. This work is necessary for us all if we are to find, if not resolution, perhaps a greater attentiveness to the viscerality of the wounds we all carry.

In many ways, this book has stemmed from our own friendship and the recognition of the necessity of building relationships within and beyond the spaces and relationships within which we work.[4] As many of our authors have highlighted, their own vulnerability has been made legible through others' vulnerability. Many of the authors here have explored the complexities of friendships, particularly as they relate to the field, to research, and to grief. Friendship in the field has been studied, theorized, scrutinized, troubled, appreciated, and celebrated within academic writing.[5] It is in these fleeting glances of relationships—some half built and often more—that multiple worldviews colliding come into view.[6] Ruptures in the pat academic frames within which researchers are trained, guided, and molded help to both make sense of the senselessness of subjectivities that are removed from taken-for-granted compunctions and further complicate our individual roles within and alongside the academy, activist communities, and sites of social service. Deep emotional relationships are often part of or even the essence of the work itself, and yet are, at times (usually?), written out of the work, framed as tangential to the project in order to maintain a kind of objective professionalism.

These rich and variegated interpersonal relationships both add to and muddle our roles as researchers, as academics, as activists, as members of social movements, as individual beings. Given the headily unmanageable power structures that come into play in research—often unbidden, often underappreciated, always complex—notions of friendship or even of being in caring relation to one another are elusive and often confused. Regardless, beneath this complexity is a mode of caring (mutuality, respect, trust, relationality)—one that is held deeply, that both drives and stymies the research and fieldwork in which so many academics and practitioners engage. Within this web of fraught relations of care, friendship, and the constraints of performing a particular kind of neoliberal subject, we offer this collection as a point of connection and solidarity with those who may find resonances with the stories told here.

To this end, this book has been part labor (and expression) of love, part call to resistance, part invitation to speak. Love holds in it revolutionary possibilities for imagining worlds otherwise. It's not a topic that finds much traction in the academy, except in moments when it is theorized. Within Western and Euro-American frames, love is framed as a private matter, a personal emotion. Even in our daily lives, we don't tend to talk about love unless we're looking for it, or we've lost it, or we've found it— most commonly in our closest relationships with friends and family of both the human and nonhuman animal varieties. Put another way, love is marginalized; and, we have asked our authors and readers to come with us to this margin because, as bell hooks tells us, it is here that we find radical openness—the site of radical possibility.[7]

It is here that communities of resistance spring up. Resistance to the silencing. And resistance to the external and internal disciplining that takes place in confronting and expressing our emotions, our grief. Thich Nhất Hạnh states:

> Resistance, at root, I think, must mean more than resistance against war. It is a resistance against all kinds of things that are like war. Because living in modern society, one feels that one cannot easily retain integrity, wholeness. One is robbed permanently of humanness, the capacity of being oneself.... So perhaps, first of all, resistance means opposition to being invaded, occupied, assaulted, and destroyed by the system. The purpose of resistance, here, is to seek the healing of yourself in order to be able to see clearly.... I think that communities of resistance should be places where people can return to themselves more easily, where the conditions are such that they can heal themselves and recover their wholeness.[8]

To insist on living from a place of love, to build communities of resistance (rather than fortresses of denial) requires that we are first honest and open with ourselves about what and how we are feeling and about how those feelings may be transforming us. To build communities of resistance from a place of love also requires that we share and connect—that we speak these truths so that others can know, hold space for, and relate to what we are feeling.

To speak these truths is to break the silence, to disrupt the comfortability of reserved performances of a-emotionality that are so deeply ingrained within late liberal capitalist societies of the global minority and that are so deeply embedded within research and fieldwork. Silence and silencing are disciplinary technologies that disallow an emotional wholeness. Continuing to be silent (or even insisting on a silence) can enact precisely the kinds of violence that we seek to undo through our work, our activism, and our communities. Thus, a refocusing on grief can work against these erasures and politicize the embodied effects of (and emotional responses to) the violent structures we study.

Expressions of grief and vulnerability, of brokenness, of harm, then, become dangerous to the very regimes that discipline. These expressions mark a politics of refusal: a refusal to be silent, a refusal to suffer in isolation, a refusal to be pathologized for these modes of deep feeling, and a refusal to pretend that the work we do doesn't radically change us.

This change can at times be constructive, generating creative approaches to thinking through and *with* the pain, grief, and disruption. At other times, these transformative experiences slow or halt our ability to move forward within the confines of neoliberal timelines. Elspeth Probyn argues that in writing about shame (and, we would add, grief), "the body becomes the battleground where ideas and experiences collide, sometimes to produce new visions of life."[9] To ignore the embodied emotional experiences—grief, shame, anger, guilt—that stem from the work that so many of us do is to individualize and sequester the very catalysts for change that often make our work meaningful. "It is time to smash the walls of pretense, shame, and silence to really show ourselves—and not just as victims of oppression, but with the motivation of communicating great feelings of caring for others and hopefulness about organizing for change, about letting our true power and brilliance guide our movement in order to recapture our full humanity in an oppressive society."[10] And we would add: not just to capture our full humanity, but our full being-ness in the broader web of human and nonhuman relationality that comprises our worlds. For, ours is a project of deep care and feeling for and with the many multispecies others and ecosystems with whom our lives and deaths are intertwined. It is a project of speaking truth to power—or, rather, of *speaking truth to pain* so that we might rupture the forces that produce that pain. What it means to speak these truths must also allow for radical alterity in how these expressions manifest: in a tapestry of grief and entangled emotions; in tears or laughter; in whoops or bellows or screeches or roars; in quiet reflections communicated through a knowing glance, a gentle touch, the purring of a cat, the quiet rustle of trees.

In this spirit, this book is also an invitation to listen with an openness to acknowledging and holding space for radically different registers of feeling. We imagine listening without judgment—not through a critical lens with an eye to academic or professional engagement, but as an act of reciprocity and transformation. Following Donna McCormack, we, too, "are uncertain of where this sharing may lead. It is intimate, life-changing and involves an unforeseeable visceral, psychic and epistemological impact. The transformation in self and other and other others is powerful, unprepared for and does not promise a brighter future. Instead, all those gathered listen, share, exchange, get things wrong, try again and importantly keep on listening, talking and seeking out innovative forms of communication."[11] What might these "innovative forms of communication" look like? And how might they work together, with, or alongside traditional or professional self-care therapies (e.g., talk therapy, mindfulness practices) without falling prey to the same late liberal tendencies of individualization? Given that scholars, activists, and practitioners will continue to engage in work that subjects us to primary and secondary trauma and causes us to grieve, and that these wounds will continue to render us vulnerable and emotionally undone, how do we embody more holistic forms of caring—personally, relationally, and in the institutional structures in which we are situated (and which might themselves be the source of our harm)?[12] Drawing on our own experiences, we maintain that raw and honest communication about these impacts can be a transformative process—a sigh of relief in moments when we expect to feel isolated. Sharing these vulnerabilities provides a break—an opening—in the shell of defensiveness we construct to hide our brokenness. But it is just that: an opening, a beginning, an invitation to (perhaps) more loving and heart-centered ways of relating to one another.

NOTES

1. See, for instance, Jennifer L. Fluri and Rachel Lehr, *The Carpetbaggers of Kabul and Other American-Afghan Entanglements: Intimate Development, Geopolitics, and the Currency of Gender and Grief* (Athens: University of Georgia Press, 2017).

2. Kenneth J. Doka, "Disenfranchised Grief," in *Living with Grief: Loss in Later Life*, ed. Kenneth J. Doka, John Breaux, and Jack D. Gordon (Washington, DC: Hospice Foundation of America, 2002), 189; see also Elizabeth Piazza-Bonin et al., "Disenfranchised Grief following African American Homicide Loss: An Inductive Case Study," *OMEGA—Journal of Death and Dying* 70, no. 4 (2015): 404–27; Lisa Marie Cacho, *Social Death: Racialized Rightlessness and the Criminalization of the Unprotected* (New York: New York University Press, 2012); Jack Santino, *Spontaneous Shrines and the Public Memorialization of Death* (New York: Palgrave Macmillan, 2016); Deborah Thien, "Emotional Geographies," in *The International Encyclopedia of Geography* (Hoboken, NJ: Wiley, 2017), 1–5.

3. Sara Ahmed, *The Cultural Politics of Emotion* (New York: Routledge, 2004).

4. Patricia J. Lopez and Kathryn Gillespie, "A Love Story: For 'Buddy System' Research in the Academy," *Gender, Place and Culture* 23, no. 12 (2016): 1689–700.

5. Kathe Browne, "Negotiations and Fieldworkings: Friendship and Feminist Research," *ACME: An International E-Journal for Critical Geographies* 2, no. 2 (2003): 132–46; Sasha Roseneil, "Why We Should Care about Friends: An Argument for Queering the Care Imaginary in Social Policy," *Social Policy and Society* 3, no. 4 (2004): 409–19; Sophie Bowlby, "Friendship, Co-presence and Care: Neglected Spaces," *Social and Cultural Geography* 12, no. 6 (2011): 605–22; Tim Bunnell et al., "Geographies of Friendships," *Progress in Human Geography* 36, no. 4 (2012): 490–507.

6. Leroy Little Bear, "Jagged Worldviews Colliding," in *Reclaiming Indigenous Voice and Vision*, ed. Marie Ann Battiste (Vancouver, BC: UBC Press, 2000), 77–85.

7. bell hooks, "Choosing the Margin as a Space of Radical Openness," in *Yearnings: Race, Gender, and Cultural Politics*, 2nd ed. (New York: Routledge, 2015).

8. Thich Nhất Hạnh, "Communities of Resistance," in *The Raft Is Not the Shore: Towards a World Where Spirituality and Politics Meet* (Maryknoll, NY: Orbis Books 2001), 129.

9. Elspeth Probyn, "Writing Shame," in *The Affect Theory Reader*, ed. Melissa Gregg and Gregory J. Seigworth (Durham, NC: Duke University Press, 2011), 89.

10. Anonymous, "For My Sister: Smashing the Walls of Pretense and Shame," in *This Bridge We Call Home: Radical Visions for Transformation*, ed. Gloria Anzaldúa and AnaLouise Keating (New York: Routledge, 2002), 295.

11. Donna McCormack, *Queer Postcolonial Narratives and the Ethics of Witnessing* (New York: Bloomsbury Academic, 2015), 23.

12. Victoria Lawson, "Instead of Radical Geography, How about Caring Geography?," *Antipode* 41, no. 1 (2009): 210–13; Joan C. Tronto, *Caring Democracy: Markets, Equality, and Justice* (New York: New York University Press, 2013).

BIBLIOGRAPHY

Ahmed, Sara. *The Cultural Politics of Emotion*. New York: Routledge, 2004.

Anonymous. "For My Sister: Smashing the Walls of Pretense and Shame." In *This Bridge We Call Home: Radical Visions for Transformation*, edited by Gloria Anzaldúa and AnaLouise Keating, 295. New York: Routledge, 2002.

Bowlby, Sophie. "Friendship, Co-presence and Care: Neglected Spaces." *Social and Cultural Geography* 12, no. 6 (2011): 605–22.

Browne, Kathe. "Negotiations and Fieldworkings: Friendship and Feminist Research." *ACME: An International E-Journal for Critical Geographies* 2, no. 2 (2003): 132–46.

Bunnell, Tim, Sallie Yea, Linda Peake, Tracey Skelton, and Monica Smith. "Geographies of Friendships." *Progress in Human Geography* 36, no. 4 (2012): 490–507.

Cacho, Lisa Marie. *Social Death: Racialized Rightlessness and the Criminalization of the Unprotected*. New York: New York University Press, 2012.

Doka, Kenneth J. "Disenfranchised Grief." In *Living with Grief: Loss in Later Life*, edited by Kenneth J. Doka, John Breaux, and Jack D. Gordon, 159–68. Washington, DC: Hospice Foundation of America, 2002.

Fluri, Jennifer L., and Rachel Lehr. *The Carpetbaggers of Kabul and Other American-Afghan Entanglements: Intimate Development, Geopolitics, and the Currency of Gender and Grief*. Athens: University of Georgia Press, 2017.

hooks, bell. *Yearning: Race, Gender, and Cultural Politics*. 2nd ed. New York: Routledge, 2015.

Lawson, Victoria. "Instead of Radical Geography, How about Caring Geography?" *Antipode* 41, no. 1 (2009): 210–13.

Little Bear, Leroy. "Jagged Worldviews Colliding." In *Reclaiming Indigenous Voice and Vision*, edited by Marie Ann Battiste, 77–85. Vancouver, BC: UBC Press, 2000.

Lopez, Patricia J., and Kathryn Gillespie. "A Love Story: For 'Buddy System' Research in the Academy." *Gender, Place and Culture* 23, no. 12 (2016): 1689–700.

Lorde, Audre. "The Transformation of Silence into Action." In *I Am Your Sister: Collected and Unpublished Writings of Audre Lorde*, edited by Rudolph P. Byrd, Johnnetta B. Cole, and Beverly Guy-Sheftall, 39–43. Oxford: Oxford University Press, 2011.

McCormack, Donna. *Queer Postcolonial Narratives and the Ethics of Witnessing.* New York: Bloomsbury Academic, 2015.

Nhất Hạnh, Thich, and Daniel Berrigan. *The Raft Is Not the Shore: Towards a World Where Spirituality and Politics Meet.* Maryknoll, NY: Orbis Books 2001.

Piazza-Bonin, Elizabeth, Robert A. Neimeyer, Laurie A. Burke, Meghan E. McDevitt-Murphy, and Amanda Young. "Disenfranchised Grief following African American Homicide Loss: An Inductive Case Study." *OMEGA—Journal of Death and Dying* 70, no. 4 (2015): 404–27.

Probyn, Elspeth. "Writing Shame." In *The Affect Theory Reader,* edited by Melissa Gregg and Gregory J. Seigworth, 71–90. Durham, NC: Duke University Press, 2011.

Roseneil, Sasha. "Why We Should Care about Friends: An Argument for Queering the Care Imaginary in Social Policy." *Social Policy and Society* 3, no. 4 (2004): 409–19.

Santino, Jack. *Spontaneous Shrines and the Public Memorialization of Death.* New York: Palgrave Macmillan, 2016.

Thien, Deborah. "Emotional Geographies." In *The International Encyclopedia of Geography,* 1–5. Hoboken, NJ: Wiley, 2017.

Tronto, Joan. *Caring Democracy: Markets, Equality, and Justice.* New York: New York University Press, 2013.

CONTRIBUTORS

Elan Abrell is a 2017–18 Farmed Animal Law and Policy Fellow at the Harvard Animal Law and Policy Program. He holds a PhD in Anthropology from the CUNY Graduate Center and a JD from UC Berkeley School of Law. His research focuses on animal rescue and care in North America, as well as other efforts to reduce animal suffering and the deleterious environmental effects of animal-based industries. He has conducted ethnographic research (funded by a grant from the National Science Foundation) on the US animal sanctuary movement, and his work has appeared in *Animals, Biopolitics, Law: Lively Legalities* and the 2017 sanctuaries-themed special issue of the *Animal Studies Journal*, which he also guest edited.

Jessie Hanna Clark is an Assistant Professor in Geography at the University of Nevada. Dr. Clark received her PhD in Geography from the University of Arizona in 2012. Her research on gender, development, and security in Kurdish Turkey has been published in several books and journals, including *Annals of the American Association of Geographers; Gender, Place and Culture;* and *Geopolitics.*

Dana Cuomo is an Assistant Professor in the Department of Diversity and Community Studies at Western Kentucky University. Her research draws on her employment experiences as a victim advocate to examine the spatialities of injustice mediated through the law, with a focus on institutional responses to gender-based violence. Dana has published in *Geopolitics*; *Social and Cultural Geography*; *Progress in Human Geography*; and *Gender, Place and Culture*.

Kalli F. Doubleday is a doctoral candidate in the Department of Geography and the Environment at the University of Texas at Austin. Her research on the human dimensions of large carnivore conservation has been published in *Geoforum*; *Conservation and Society*; and *Animals and Society*. These works utilize the theoretical lens of animal geography combined with the axioms of conservation biology to study conservation ethics, media coverage, and rewilding of leopards and tigers in South Asia.

María Elena García is an Associate Professor in the Comparative History of Ideas program and the Jackson School of International Studies at the University of Washington. She received her PhD in anthropology at Brown University and has been a Mellon Fellow at Wesleyan University and Tufts University. Her first book, *Making Indigenous Citizens: Identities, Development, and Multicultural Activism in Peru* (2005), examines Indigenous and intercultural politics in Peru. Her work on indigeneity and interspecies politics in the Andes has appeared in multiple edited volumes and journals such as *Anthropology Now*; *Anthropological Quarterly*; *International Journal of Bilingual Education and Bilingualism*; *Journal of Latin American and Caribbean Anthropology*; *Latin American Perspectives*; and *Latin American and Caribbean Ethnic Studies*. Her second book project, "Culinary Spectacles: Gastro-Politics, and Other Tales of Race and Species in Peru," examines the intersections of race, species, and capital in contemporary Peru.

David Boarder Giles is a Lecturer in Anthropology at Deakin University in Melbourne, Australia. He writes about cultural economies of waste and homelessness, and the politics of urban food security and public space, particularly in "global" cities. He is the author of the forthcoming book *"A Mass Conspiracy to Feed People": World-Class Waste and the Struggle for the Global City*.

Kathryn Gillespie is a feminist geographer and critical animal studies scholar. She has published in *Gender, Place and Culture*; *Antipode*; and *Hypatia* and is the author of *The Cow with Ear Tag #1389*.

Jenny R. Isaacs is a doctoral candidate within the Department of Geography at Rutgers University. She is a critical human-environment geographer focused on biodiversity preservation in contexts of crisis, currently researching the challenges of long-distance migratory species conservation. Her research combines feminist-informed science and technology studies, posthuman political ecology, conservation biogeography, and archipelagic studies. Using institutional ethnography, discourse analysis, and praxiography, her dissertation, "Tracing the Shorebird Conservation Network," specifically focuses on the political ecology of the Western Hemisphere Shorebird Reserve Network along the Atlantic flyway, framing it as an emerging "conservation archipelago."

Patricia J. Lopez is an Assistant Professor of Geography at Dartmouth College. Her work centers on care ethics, health citizenship, and humanitarianism. She has published in *Gender, Place and Culture* and *Environment and Planning A* and has published an edited volume, *Economies of Death*, with Kathryn Gillespie.

Avril Maddrell is an Associate Professor at the University of Reading. She is a social and cultural geographer interested in historical and contemporary issues. Research interests include gender; emotional-affective geographies; deathscapes; sacred mobilities; place, landscape, and heritage; historiography; and charity shops as sociocultural spaces. She is a coeditor of *Gender, Place and Culture* and *Social and Cultural Geography*.

Abigail H. Neely is an Assistant Professor of Geography at Dartmouth College. She has conducted ethnographic research in three communities in Pholela, South Africa, since 2006, exploring questions of health, healing, and nature-society relationships. She is just beginning a new project on death and dying in twenty-first-century South Africa. She has published in *Progress in Human Geography*; *Journal of Southern African Studies*; and *Annals of the American Association of Geographers* and currently has a forthcoming book titled *Lives, Labor, and Witchcraft: Reimagining Social Medicine from the South*.

Elizabeth Olson is an Associate Professor of Geography and Global Studies at the University of North Carolina at Chapel Hill. Her interests are broadly encompassed by ethics, care, and young people—often in relation to the production and experience of inequality. Her recent research has focused on understanding historical and contemporary caregiving by young people in the United States.

William J. Payne is a doctoral candidate in Critical Human Geography (York University), teaches part-time in York's Department of Geography and in George Brown College's Community Worker Program, and is associated with the Centre for Research on Latin America and the Caribbean and with the Centre for Refugee Studies. William researches the violation of the human rights of sexual/gender minorities in contexts marked by organized violence and impunity, and has published several book chapters and journal articles, including in the journal *Gender, Place and Culture*. William also has extensive experience as a human rights worker in Mexico, Colombia, Canada, and Palestine.

Amy Spark is an environmental scientist and advocate in Alberta, Canada, specializing in the intersection between ecological and mental health. She holds an MSc in Environment, Culture and Society with Distinction from the University of Edinburgh, where she was awarded Best Overall Contribution to the Programme. Amy is an amateur urban homesteader, outdoors enthusiast, budding writer, and lover of science fiction.

Yolanda Valencia is a doctoral candidate in the Department of Geography at the University of Washington, Seattle. In the summer of 2017 she had the opportunity to publish two significant articles that relate to im/migration, politics, and race in *Gender, Place and Culture* and the *Journal of Latin American Geography*. She has been granted a Dissertation Writing Fellowship by the Graduate Opportunities and Minority Achievement Program (GO-MAP) for the year 2017–18.

Cleo Woelfle-Erskine is Assistant Professor of Equity and Environmental Justice at the School of Marine and Environmental Affairs at the University of Washington, Seattle, where he researches human relations to rivers and their multispecies inhabitants. Trained in ecology, hydrology, geomorphology, critical social science, and feminist science and technology studies, he facilitates collaborative research in partnership with tribes, agencies, citizen scientists, and local community members. He is a coeditor of and contributor to *Dam Nation: Dispatches from the Water Underground* and author of a manuscript in progress, titled "Underflow: Transfiguring Riverine Relations, Imagining Queer-Trans Ecologies," which considers the lingering presences of Manifest Destiny (ecological, socioscientific, and psychological) and the ways that this injurious "destiny" can be transfigured and overturned to renew human-water-fish relations.

INDEX